CAREERS IN

This book is due for return on or before the last date shown below.

CAREERS IN
MARKETING, ADVERTISING and PUBLIC RELATIONS

Adela Stanley

eighth edition

KOGAN PAGE

First published in 1980 as *Careers in Marketing, Public Relations and Advertising*

Eighth edition, 2003

Kogan Page Limited
120 Pentonville Road
London N1 9JN
United Kingdom
www.kogan-page.co.uk

© Kogan Page Ltd, 2003

British Library Cataloguing in Publication Data

A CIP record for this book is available from the British Library.

ISBN 0 7494 3917 3

Typeset by Jean Cussons Typesetting, Diss, Norfolk
Printed and bound in Great Britain by Clays Ltd, St Ives plc

Contents

Acknowledgements

I wish to thank the staff of Brompton Library, who are still better than the Internet, Dr Simon Gallacher of the Institute of Direct Marketing, and all the friends in the advertising, marketing and PR industry who helped with information, advice and anecdotes.

Introduction

Marketing, advertising and public relations (PR) touch people's lives around the world. Watch TV news footage of refugees receiving aid; they often know what Pampers and Coca-Cola mean, even if they don't speak English. Coca-Cola, Kellogg's, McDonald's, Kodak, Marlboro, IBM, American Express, Sony, Mercedes-Benz and Nescafé are generally the world's ten top-selling brands – and they reach and retain their position by the efforts of their marketing and advertising departments. This is a vibrant, interesting and exciting industry – which means thousands of applicants for every available job.

Looking for a job in this industry may seem foolhardy to some people – it has a reputation for being difficult to get into, easy to get the sack from and with a fairly tough ride in between. But you wouldn't be reading this book if you didn't feel that you had something to offer – so I hope to help you find a career.

First, to get a job you must show commitment to and understanding of the industry. When you pick up your favourite magazine, don't flick through the ads – analyse each one. Who is advertising aimed at? What is the message? Does this come across to YOU? If you had the money, would you buy the product? And how and where can you buy the product?

In this book we will be discussing real-life situations and mentioning brand names. Some are household names; others, while they may be new to you, have a unique way of promoting their product. When shopping, what are you buying? Why? Do you choose a product because its marketing, advertising or PR is effective for you? Every ad has a story to tell. Each time you make a choice and you buy a product, the marketing gurus have been there before you to help you make this choice. Even if you swear you don't normally look at ads, the PR industry will keep you aware of what is happening.

We mention many brands in this book; we can't mention every company that has a marketing, advertising and PR strategy, and the reason why some companies are mentioned is that their name comes readily to mind to illustrate a point.

This book looks at marketing, advertising and PR separately because, whilst a smaller organisation may have one marketing person to carry out all the advertising, PR and marketing activities, larger companies and agencies have specific people for each role.

Marketing is mainly buying and selling – goods, ideas, money – and all the processes this entails. Marketing is said to be about understanding what consumers want and how their needs can be satisfied.

Advertising is a part of the broader marketing process, as are sales, market research, sales promotion, PR and many other disciplines. If you are working in marketing you may well cover all aspects of the process in your work, perhaps in the marketing department of a manufacturing company; or you may specialise in one tiny part, as an account executive for a sales promotion agency.

What is PR? It is a way of promoting a product or service by using the media, at an event, etc, to ensure the product is well thought of by users and buyers.

These are stimulating and exciting work areas which, for the right sort of person, can make work seem more like play. In some ways it is – if your idea of fun is constant contact with people, using your charm and powers of persuasion and being creative at the same time. Many advertising and PR agencies, marketing departments, sales promotion agencies, etc have a creative and dynamic atmosphere that suits some people down to the ground. Others would find it claustrophobic, noisy, undisciplined and very hard work. Signing up for a career in this industry means devoting much of your life to your job.

Other marketing-related jobs are more low-key – some demand good communicating skills and a high volume of writing output. There is much planning and serious back-room work to be done, with analysis and systems work. You need to find out what sort of people work in these areas and decide whether you are one of them.

So, is marketing really such a difficult profession to enter? Are there any jobs? Are organisations making marketing any sort of priority today? To answer the last question first: yes, marketing is thriving in the current marketplace. There are jobs for good people. Indeed, there is a shortfall of trained staff in certain areas.

In recent years, many organisations have been hit by a downturn in the economy, and many of the most spectacular (or at least the best-publicised) falls were within advertising agencies. Many agencies had thriving graduate training programmes, highly paid staff and top salaries reaching levels that we can now only gasp at. The reduction in business caused many to downsize, stop training and say goodbye to some of the highest earners, with appropriate reductions all the way through. Now that the economy is healthy again, agencies face serious personnel shortages, with not enough staff coming through. Some agencies are finding the problem of getting good trained staff so acute that they are turning away business.

Agencies always looked for the very best graduates for their training schemes. Since the appalling publicity the economically depressed agencies received in recent years, they are not always perceived as the best place to make a career. Recruiters looking for their usual graduates are alarmed to find that many now want to go into more secure careers in the City.

In mainstream marketing, demand at all levels is good, with some organisations investing once more in training new graduates. Indeed, organisations find themselves in an increasingly competitive world and appreciate the importance of communication – to staff, existing customers and the general trade and public communities, as well as specific target groups – more than ever. At one time, 'marketing' was something that went on in large commercial companies trying to sell a product or service. Nowadays, it is everywhere – in schools and colleges, local and central government, charities, and consumer groups. For an organisation to thrive it needs marketing. And so marketing needs more people.

Within the newly thriving marketing business certain areas are gaining in importance. Sales promotion (the use of consumer, trade and sales force incentives) is growing rapidly because it is flexible, specific and cost-effective. Along the same lines (understanding the importance of targeting the correct market), market research is also gaining in importance. The use of design in the marketing process is being taken more seriously, with the image of an organisation seen as worth spending millions of pounds on.

If you are thinking of a career in any of these areas, you will find a reasonable amount of information available to you on specific qualifications, but guidance on how to get a job can be frustratingly vague. Although qualifications are important, and increasingly so, there is still that element of 'being in the right place at the right time' and having that 'something extra' about you. Networking still plays a big part in recruitment.

Jobseekers who paraded outside advertising agencies with sandwich boards saying 'I'm the person you are looking for' are now part of recruitment folklore. The marketing industries take on people who can demonstrate a genuine interest in the job through having the right qualifications and appropriate work experience. If you really are the most amazingly creative individual but have little to show for it on paper, you may possibly succeed; but most of us need a curriculum vitae that demonstrates a genuine determination to become a marketing professional.

This book is intended to give school, college and university leavers, people who have been made redundant, women returners or second careerists an idea of the opportunities in marketing, advertising and PR, the qualifications necessary to find work, and some hints on getting there. This is a jargon-filled industry, so I hope the glossary will be useful.

Finally, you are already a consumer and therefore a target for advertising and marketing. Start analysing just what makes you buy certain goods regularly and what makes you buy on impulse. Understanding how and why you buy products will help you understand this fascinating industry.

Top Tips

If you want to get into the industry

◆ Be prepared to work long hours.
◆ 'Live the product'. You can't enthuse over a product unless you use, understand, know and believe in it.
◆ Read and compare ads in newspapers and magazines.
◆ Watch ads on TV.
◆ Look out for eye-catching posters.
◆ Keep your ears and eyes open when out shopping.
◆ Listen to what people say when they recommend products to friends.
◆ Think what friends and family buy, and why.
◆ Start asking around for suitable work experience.

A great example of the power of marketing, advertising and public relations is the New Covent Garden Soup Company, whose Kate Kime admits that the company was 'built on the back of PR', launching into a market dominated by Heinz and Campbells' tinned soups. The soup was packaged in cartons and needed to be sold from chilled cabinets because the ingredients were fresh. Targeting 'well-educated' customers, the company has since gone from strength to strength, and is now opening soup bars.

With the help of this book, and perseverance, you could be part of similar success stories.

Good luck!

2 Marketing

So what is marketing?

It is often claimed that advertising, PR, market research etc come under the umbrella of marketing. The Chartered Institute of Marketing (CIM) say: 'Marketing is the management process which identifies, anticipates and supplies customer requirements efficiently and profitably.'

There is no one definition of marketing that describes it as it is used in every organisation. It can:

◆ identify customer needs;
◆ determine the best way of getting customers to buy products;
◆ ensure products are available when and where customers want;
◆ tell customers about the existence and features of the product;
◆ decide on price;
◆ ensure after-sales service is of the right quality.

Market research identifies potential customer requirements; new product development produces the required item; advertising (and PR where appropriate) communicates to the customer what is available; and below-the-line promotions and sales get the product or service to the customer.

Below-the-line marketing is increasingly important; many companies go out to specialist agencies to set up call centres, run special promotions, handle incentives, organise exhibition stands and carry out direct mailing.

In- and out-of-house work

Many larger companies have people within their organisation (in-house) carrying out marketing and PR. However, these companies can buy in the services of professional agencies (out-of-house) who are specialists, taking the 'brief' from the client (the organisation) and staying in close contact through regular meetings.

Organisations decide how much they do in- and out-of-house for various reasons: quality of available specialists, type of work required, budget and regularity of the work. Many large organisations use a combination of in- and out-of-house experts, with their marketing manager being responsible for appointing and monitoring the work of the agency.

This book discusses in-house jobs and agency positions. Many people move between the two, working within an organisation and then moving to a senior position in an agency or vice versa. The greatest difference between them is probably that in-house, you are working as part of a team towards a common corporate goal, whereas in an agency, you could be working on several different accounts (for different clients), each demanding your attention.

If you would prefer to get into general marketing (as opposed to a specific advertising or PR job), you need to know about the other areas described later in this book, but you won't necessarily be expected to have all the specific skills needed by an executive in a PR consultancy or a market researcher in an advertising agency.

Since general marketing combines advertising and public relations activities, this chapter will be useful to anybody thinking of going into these specialist areas.

The process of marketing

There are two kinds of product that can be created for sale:

- **Manufactured goods.** Examples of manufactured goods are shoes, books and cars.
- **Services.** Services include banking, management consultancy and tourism.

The role of marketing in the creation and sale of products is to work out what people want or will buy, ensuring that the product is right for these people, then making sure that it is available at the right price in the right places.

For example, there would be no point in making a car with a built-in perfume dispenser if market research showed that this was low on the priorities list of car-buyers. However, a car with safety features would be a popular buy, as long as it was offered at a price people were prepared to pay, readily available and promoted to potential customers (through advertising).

So, marketing means taking steps to ensure that the product sells. In many organisations today, marketing is a business philosophy that is applied to everything they do.

The marketing department

The structure and responsibilities of a marketing department within an organisation vary according to the organisation's size and the importance it places on marketing.

In a large firm, for example, the marketing director will have a say in all the company's activities; he or she will be on the board of directors and involved in important decisions, from deciding on new products to whether to buy up a competitor.

A team of managers will work under the director on different product 'lines'. They are often called 'brand managers'. They specialise in a certain product or range and deal with the advertising, public relations and sales promotion activities for that product. Some of these services may be found in-house whilst others are bought in from out-of-house. These managers will have support staff in the form of 'executives' and 'assistants'.

Marketing a new product

To understand how a marketing department functions, look at this example of a new 'fast-moving consumer good' (FMCG) as it is conceived and launched, pinpointing where the marketing department is involved.

In this example, drinks manufacturer Fizz Inc. is interested in producing a new soft drink. There are many similar products, so the company has to ensure it can win enough customers – perhaps 'stealing' market share from other companies with established brands.

Market research

Fizz Inc. first wants to find out as much as possible about the market for a new drink. The marketing manager for this new brand decides to use an out-of-house market research agency and briefs it. The agency may use a combination of statistics and reports that are already available, as well as tailor-made research, to collect more specific information. It provides Fizz Inc. with a detailed report that concludes that there is a 'gap in the market' for a low sugar fizzy high fruit juice content drink, aimed at the 24–30 age group, who are prepared to pay a higher price for a non-alcoholic drink if they felt it was doing them good.

New product development

After 12 months of laboratory work and 'tastings', the research and development department (R&D), working with the marketing manager, comes up with the right blend for the new drink. The marketing director conducts a 'brainstorm' to decide on the all-important name, and a selection of possibles is fed through the market research system once again. 'Arcadian Spring' is born!

Closely connected is packaging research and design: with so many similar products on supermarket shelves, this one has to stand out. Different bottles are tested by the market research agency, and the company decides on a tall glass bottle with a silver label, to give a sleek, sophisticated image that will not look out of place beside a wine bottle.

Advertising

Fizz Inc. uses various advertising agencies on its different brands. The marketing manager wants to make sure that the right agency is working on this important new launch, so she puts the account out to tender (invites a selection of agencies to 'pitch' for the work). Each agency offers an impressive presentation for the product launch campaign and one is selected. (See Chapter 3 for further information about advertising agency pitching and the production of an advertising campaign.)

The successful agency now works closely with the marketing department to plan the launch campaign. It will have suggested to Fizz Inc. any further market research it believes to be necessary in order to make sure that the advertising message, as well as the product itself, is absolutely right.

The launch process

Fizz Inc. has to launch and promote Arcadian Spring to different audiences, with slightly different messages:

◆ Fizz Inc.'s team of sales representatives who sell Fizz Inc. products to shops, wholesalers, restaurant and pub chains;
◆ retailers;
◆ consumers.

The sales team is provided with glossy promotional material, sales targets with prizes for those who reach their top sales figures and an impressive presentation at the annual sales conference.

Retailers are provided with free 'point of sale' (POS) display material, sales promotion incentives to stock the new drink (prizes, weekends away, etc) and a presentation by the sales team to persuade them to buy large stocks for the launch. They also need to know how the new product will be supported by advertising and sales promotion activities, since there is little point in buying stock if there is nothing to make customers buy.

Consumers are bombarded with advertising about Arcadian Spring. The advertising agency has produced a series of television advertisements to be shown around 9pm (peak time for the target audience). Radio advertising will run concurrently. Full-page colour ads will be run in women's magazines and colour supplements of the Sunday newspapers.

PR

Fizz Inc.'s PR agency has organised a press launch, with a leading sports personality as guest speaker. Press releases and samples of Arcadian Spring have been distributed and advertorials booked in magazines.

Sales promotion

Incentives offered to retailers and wholesalers to encourage them to stock the product are part of a sales promotion strategy. Incentives can also be used at other times during the 'life cycle' of the product. If sales began to flag after a successful launch, new promotions could be devised to increase sales: perhaps 'money off' vouchers, or Fizz Inc. could link up with a yoghurt manufacturer and run a series of healthy eating and drinking promotional articles in a magazine. The opportunities are endless, and it takes a creative mind and some good research to devise the campaign that will prove the most successful.

The marketing manager

The marketing manager has coordinated this activity. The launch of a major new consumer product can take years, although manufacturers are now having to work faster to avoid a competitor launching a rival product first. The planning process is critically important: many of the activities described briefly above take months to prepare; and there are controlling bodies, such as the Advertising Standards Authority (ASA), which have to approve different types of advertising before they are used.

Sales

There is no point performing all these functions if there is no salesforce (except in areas such as direct mail or marketing, when the customer responds to carefully geared promotional literature and needs no additional persuasion). Although sales is not strictly a branch of marketing, they are often grouped together as 'Sales and Marketing'. However, it is important to consider sales as part of, or parallel to, the marketing process, especially in career terms, as many marketing training programmes ask their trainees to spend time 'at the sharp end' (sales) first. Many people go into sales as a way into marketing, advertising and so on, in areas such as selling advertising space. Some enjoy selling so much they decide to stay there.

Launching Arcadian Spring, the marketing manager is in close liaison with the sales manager at all stages in the marketing process. The salesforce have first-hand experience of the customer, and feedback is invaluable in the research stages.

What kind of people work in marketing?

You need an all-round understanding of how the business operates, since your work is central to most of the company's activities, dealing closely with sales, manufacturing, R&D, credit control and order processing. Moreover, while marketing makes demands on your creative and interpersonal skills, you need to analyse and use large quantities of financial and market research information; such skills are increasingly sought after by companies recruiting for their marketing departments.

You have to be able to plan in a structured way and think creatively, whilst working irregular hours, at weekends and under pressure, keeping to tight deadlines. No matter how carefully marketing plans are devised and timetables drawn up, there will always be times when a confirmation to go ahead is late in coming, a new design isn't agreed until the last minute or a competitor makes a move – meaning last-minute changes in briefs for the advertising and PR agencies, changes to the promotional packs for retailers or even a complete redesign of the product.

Forward planning is extremely important. It is often said that a marketing job is never finished. There is always more to be done, so setting out objectives, strategies and tactics within budgets, followed by their execution and analysing the results, have to be performed carefully and accurately. It is easy to be diverted, although you still need to be able to spot a genuine opportunity if one arises and rearrange priorities around it.

Understanding consumer needs is a key quality. Whilst market research offers accurate information about when, how and why people make purchasing decisions, it is not infallible, and you have to have that 'instinctive feel' about a product to be successful.

One of the benefits of working within a company's marketing department is that you may be dealing with external agencies: advertising, PR or sales promotion. This is an excellent way of finding out what people in these service companies do, and whether you might be interested in specialising in one of those areas.

To get a feel for the qualities employers are looking for, read recruitment advertisements in the trade press. (See Chapter 9.)

Marketing on the Internet (see Chapter 7) is a growing sector. In the late 1990s, Prudential Banking launched Egg, which it called 'a radically different direct financial organisation'. It looked for people who:

- had the ability to plan and organise;
- paid attention to detail;
- had communication skills;

◆ had analytical skills;
◆ were team players;
◆ were able to work on their own initiative.

Market research

Major market research companies often use temporary staff for surveys, providing useful work experience. One good example of this is in tourism, the second largest industry in Britain. One of the largest annual surveys is carried out by temporary staff working at airports and ports around Britain, questioning visitors on their experiences. This information can then be used by tourism companies to plan future developments, new attractions, etc.

Building for the future

Legislation banning cigarette advertising means tobacco companies are diversifying into other markets such as travel and luxury goods: clothes, cosmetics and skin-care (turnover of Dunhill's luxury goods now exceeds their tobacco sales). It is more than likely your first job could be working on a 'luxury product' account, especially as the industry is an enormous spender on advertising and marketing.

Marketing to potential customers for luxury goods requires a high degree of customer care. For example, instead of hiring a team of demonstrators to promote and sell a new product for a few days, cosmetic companies employ full-time demonstrators, calling them in for training on new products.

Cosmetic companies used to market 'dream creams', wrapping products in glossy packaging. Then came Anita Roddick with her Body Shop products. It is no coincidence that, with an expected downturn from advertising and sales of tobacco, French, Swiss and Japanese companies and investors saw the potential of 'greener' skin-care, and today, UK cosmetic counters are dominated by Continental companies such as Sisley, La Prairie, Guerlain and Clarins.

Whilst men and women are increasingly prepared to pay for quality skin products, they tend to spend more on better products and less on cheap impulse purchases. Even Chanel, once relying on the glamour of its name to sell products, has recently invested heavily in a new research laboratory. Giant US companies now follow the Continental lead: Estée Lauder's PX Prescriptives range is backed up by medical and scientific research, with costs going into the ingredients rather than on packaging. Continental marketing, with 'try and buy' free samples, is being used effectively by Clarins in the UK.

When YOU buy skin-care or perfume, watch how marketing relies on highly trained sales teams. Natalie Buckley, PR of Swiss company La Prairie, says today's customers definitely know what they want, asking searching questions about ingredients and properties.

Pre-interview research

Read anything written by the 'serious' beauty editors, such as Newby Hands, and study the cosmetic counters of your local department store for the cutting edge of promotion. Listen in as staff talk about their company's products. Instead of telling customers how the product will make them look, they are more likely to do a skin analysis, stressing long-term benefits of skin creams, so building customer loyalty and repeat sales.

Coco Chanel was the first to promote a suntan as a beauty accessory; 60 years later, advisers are trained to help customers understand cellular skin treatment systems for skin protection and the importance of the sun protection factor (SPF) – La Prairie says products must contain a minimum SPF 15 for outdoors. Continental women still like a suntanned look, but their suntans are glorious 'fake' foundations from Guerlain and Sisley, rather than the sun.

Notice how simple the packaging used by market leaders is. PX Prescriptives' bestselling 'Comfort' cream is an extremely effective product sold in a very simple jar, and its 'Vibrant' cream, a favourite anti-jet lag product with businesswomen and models, is also packaged simply. Look at Sisley, which also uses very plain packaging, even though it is increasing its market share with ecological compounds for day and night use, on their own or underneath other creams.

Top Tips

◆ The companies mentioned above will often do a free in-store make-up; have a session before your interview – it's a great morale booster.

◆ Remember staff's sales patter when asked questions at interview!

Word-of-mouth

AB consumers are strong on word-of-mouth, so up-market cosmetic companies such as Kanebo tailor marketing to take advantage of this. When they launched their Sensai Cellular Advanced Recovery Concentrate, clients were given technical details of how stress unbalances the skin: 'as a result skin cells forget how to be perfect'. Details of how scientists had produced a concentrate to 're-programme cellular activity' were technical, but Kanebo know that their businesswomen clients want to know and are prepared to pay for top research, if the creams work.

Instead of advertising, Kanebo hand out samples, telling clients to use these on one side of the face only and compare the difference. It must work, as women queue to buy their top-selling La Crème at £360 a jar.

What next?

There has been a quiet masculine revolution – Boots, for example, is opening 'men only' skin-care departments. Clarins was surprised when market research said women were buying their products for boyfriends. Clarins was one of the first companies to use plant extracts in a big way, and its products are generally fragrance-free and appeal to men – who also discovered its exfoliators got rid of dead skin on their face. Clarins' bestselling 'Doux Peeling', for the face, and body exfoliators are packaged in very simple white containers that won't look out of place in a masculine – or feminine – setting.

Marketing service companies

Tourism is another section that makes extensive use of marketing expertise. Luxury 4-star individually owned hotels band together to market themselves in the consortium Relais et Chateaux; upmarket B&Bs market themselves as 'Wolsey Lodges'. To promote their properties, owners of stately homes go to a marketing company like Consilium Heritage Marketing, whose founder, Brandon Stuart-Barker, identified a niche for marketing private venues for corporate hospitality and conferences, ranging from Trinity House, London; Newby Hall, Yorkshire; Adlington Hall, Cheshire; and Manderston, the house featured in the TV series *Edwardian Country House*.

These venues have to be marketed to a clearly defined group of buyers who are choosy, demanding and individual. To attract these people the marketing consortia take stands at trade exhibitions such as the Conference Industry Exhibition (CONFEX) at Earls Court or the European Incentive Business Travel and Meetings Exhibition (EIBTM) at Geneva, publish glossy directories to sit on top of travel agents' desks and run special promotion evenings for specially selected guests to spread the marketing message.

Case Study

Over Christmas and New Year London's hoteliers faced two weeks of empty rooms, bars and restaurants, until in 1987 the City of Westminster and its hoteliers came up with the idea for the Lord Mayor of Westminster's London Parade.

Targeting American marching bands, invitations went out to take part in a New Year's Day Parade. Normally, these bands have invitations to appear from all over the world but Westminster came up with a unique selling point (USP). Each band leader would be photographed with Westminster's Lord Mayor in his ceremonial robes. The chance to shake hands with a real British 'Lord' was irresistible! As each band marched past the saluting stand their leader stepped up to a podium to shake the Lord Mayor's hand. Photos of them shaking hands with the Lord Mayor were beamed to newspapers all over the United States.

Press officer Mark Philips says this is now the biggest event of its kind in the world, and London's hotels are filled from Christmas until after New Year with thousands of performers and their families. You may have seen photos of their cheerleaders performing spectacular somersaults high above the streets of London. Information from www.londonparade. co.uk.

Top Tips

When sun tan lotion company Malibu commissioned a report, they found that 72 per cent of those surveyed thought suncare lotions were expensive. So size of bottles was increased, offering a 30 per cent saving over buying two smaller bottles. The result was a 25 per cent growth in their market.

Case Study

Jonathan *is Senior Brand Manager for Industrial Products within a multinational food and chemical company.*

After studying French and German at university, I joined a food manufacturing company as a trainee marketing manager, spending my first year on the road as a sales representative. This was tiring and often frustrating – I used to make appointments with a retailer only to discover they weren't in that day, or that I was double-booked with somebody else! I visited retail outlets to encourage them to stock our products, telling them about the advertising we were doing, and the sales promotions we were running. A good supplier–customer relationship is better for both parties; whilst finding out why a delivery had been late, I could offer advice on displaying the product more effectively and how to make the most of the advertising we were doing. I realise now that it taught me a great deal about customer needs – particularly those of a retailer.

After a while, I decided that I would prefer to be working on less consumer-oriented products, so I moved to my current company, where I coordinate new product launches and market industrial cleaning products to hotels and hospitals. I have recently finished a product launch, and was involved at all stages of its development, from the initial market research where we and our research agency conducted jury panel interviews and in-company trials, through the product and packaging development, to the launch events and promotion to the industry.

With an industrial product, while price is still important, so is technical or service support: if a product isn't working as well as it should be, we can be on the spot within hours to try to diagnose the problem. Each customer is a major one for us and to lose one through lack of support would be a disaster. We spend a great deal of money gaining new customers so their accounts are worth a lot.

Training here has been excellent – I've been on courses to develop both my specific marketing skills and the more individual skills that still have a bearing on my work: communication, delegation and financial expertise. I would recommend anybody keen to enter the marketing department of a large company to find out as much as possible about the company, its products, its markets and its competitors. Try to get some unpaid work experience there – even if it is only filing – you can take the opportunity to learn and you might get noticed! It is also vital to have an understanding of business finance.

Oddly enough, I'm now keen to move back into working on fast-moving consumer goods (FMCG) products, but in a brand-marketing role. I want to apply my marketing research and product launch experience on a less industrial product and in a broader consumer market. Fortunately, my company produces consumer goods, too, so it is likely that I will be able to move within the organisation.

Top Tips

As a service industry, tourism relies heavily on marketing expertise. Many potential employers would rather you had a good marketing degree than one in tourism. Regional Tourist Boards, tour operators, hotels, tourist venues and many other tourism companies rely on good marketing to attract visitors.

Are you a brand ambassador?

Recently the Marketing and Communication Agency commissioned a report from MORI (a leading market research company) on why traditional marketing 'tools' – quality, price and speed to market – are no longer so effective. The research came to the conclusion that today it is the companies whose people build relationships with customers that have the commercial advantage, and named these employees 'brand ambassadors'. 41 per cent of customers surveyed said they are likely to buy a company's products again because of the way staff treat them, ahead of advertising, branding and promotions.

Perhaps in future, marketing departments will work together with personnel to create more brand ambassadors.

Top Tips

Send an sae to CIM for their excellent booklet *Getting a Job in Marketing.*

Advertising

What is advertising?

According to the Advertising Association, the advertising business covers three main types of employer organisations:

◆ advertisers (who use it);
◆ agencies (who make it);
◆ the media (who display it).

The IPA (Institute of Practitioners in Advertising) says that advertising is promoting, informing and enthusing. Even, when appropriate, pleading... to deliver pertinent and, hopefully, first-rate advertising solutions to help clients achieve their business goals.

All advertisements offer information, but many also encourage an action – often the purchase of a product or service. We see advertising in the press, on television and on hoardings, and hear it on commercial radio. What each ad attempts to do is to emphasise to its target audience the clear benefits of its product or service, in the most cost-effective way.

Top Tips

Think about the last time you bought something:

◆ Do you always buy this product?
◆ Did you buy it because you heard about it on radio or saw an ad?
◆ Was the product being demonstrated where you shopped?

Like it or hate it, advertising can influence what we buy and when. The Advertising Association says advertising is generally recognised to have practical benefits for everyone; eg large-volume sales keep prices down.

We will concentrate here on the activities of advertising agencies because, although some organisations run their own advertising campaigns, the principles and techniques of advertising can be more clearly seen through what an agency does.

Advertising agencies

An agency offers a service to companies or organisations wanting to tell consumers and interested parties about their products or services. The agency, using a combination of people with specific skills, will look at the product or service, identify its most desirable and believable benefits, and devise a campaign to communicate them to the target audience. It will offer the client a proposal suggesting the best 'media' to use (press, television, radio, in-store promotion, exhibitions and so on) and the 'message' that they have decided would be the most successful.

Some agencies are 'full service', offering a range of services, including account management, creative work, media planning, marketing research, sales promotion and PR. Other agencies may specialise in direct marketing or market research.

Top Tips

For more information on jobs see the Advertising Association's excellent booklet *Getting into Advertising*.

Account management

Account management is the overall running of the account (the business with the client) and it can be stressful! You need to be sensitive to the needs of your client, taking the brief (description of their objectives and ideas) and explaining it to those inside your agency who need to translate that into advertising. You also need to be able to liaise effectively with the agency team working on the account. The client needs regular updates on progress and will want to know how well the campaign is doing.

The creative department

The creative department is where ideas and plans are translated into visual images and words. There will be copywriters and graphic/visual artists assigned, often working in teams, to different accounts.

Copywriters think up slogans, voice-overs and any wording that will go to make up the advertisement. Whilst copywriting is a skill that can be improved with practice and training, good copywriters have a knack for finding that clever, arresting phrase and for hitting the nail on the head when it comes to stressing the benefits of this type of aftershave or that sort of personal savings account. There is much clever psychology in good advertising copy: copywriters must understand their audiences and be able to supply just the right words in the right way. Examples of copy that has proved almost timeless would be 'Roses grow on you' (for Roses chocolates) or 'Naughty but nice' (for cream cakes). It might seem as if copywriters spend much of their time gazing into space for inspiration, but there is no doubt that top copywriters have an enviable skill that can be worth a fortune.

Visualisers, **artists** and **graphic designers** employ two distinct skills: visualisers (art direction and/or design) often work closely with a writer to create original ideas, show the idea on paper and sketch the layout of an advertisement. Artists and graphic designers produce the finished artwork which will be used in the final copy.

Artists provide accurate artwork, assembling photographs, drawings, typesetting, etc to bring the visualiser's ideas to life. They often produce a storyboard (a series of cartoons containing a sketch showing the progress of a film sequence) or animatics (the film taken one step further with the worked-up sketches on film with sound).

Agency producers

Agency producers are responsible for the production of a television or film ad. This is very much like making a mini-film, and if the client is spending a great deal of money (launching a new car, for example), the sum involved has been known to be more than the cost of an entire feature film! The Guinness ad with the horses coming out of the ocean, for instance, cost more than a million pounds to make. The agency producer will invariably be working with an outside film company, and he or she will coordinate all the production personnel, location, choice of director and so on. In this area of advertising, the agency itself is buying in services from another supplier and has to obtain the best deal possible for its client.

The Economist says the top TV advertisers are:

- BT;
- Procter and Gamble;
- Procter and Gamble Health and Beauty;
- Kellogg's;
- Van den Bergh Foods;
- Mars;
- Ford;
- Elida Fabergé;
- Renault;
- Vauxhall.

Look them up in the *Advertisers Annual* (which should be in your local library) if you don't know their brands.

Marketing research and planning

These areas are closely connected. Agencies are becoming increasingly involved in the research stage of the advertising process. Sometimes, a client will have carried out extensive research to produce statistics and market analysis and will present the agency with its findings, so the agency ensures its work focuses on the type of customer, age group, demographic type and so on. In other instances, the agency will carry out the research on behalf of the client. The planner has to understand consumers and use research information in the best way possible. A good planner will have experience of analysing research and tries to keep ahead of the client by supplying them with up to the minute market information. This all contributes to good client–agency relationships.

The 'media planner' will be the person responsible for booking advertising across the range of media available. Using magazine and newspaper circulation figures and readership profiles, viewer and listener figures, and profiles for television and radio programmes, he or she will draw up a media plan matching budget and creative constraints of the campaign. He or she will be making comparisons between the different types of media:

- ◆ **Television.** Wide audiences, which can be targeted geographically. Product can be demonstrated visually and through sound. High cost.
- ◆ **Commercial radio.** Easy to target geographical locations. Smaller audiences than television. Because it is only audio, messages may not be so readily retained.
- ◆ **Cinema.** Benefit of sound and vision, but smaller audiences and more unpredictable than television.
- ◆ **Hoardings.** Depending on location, many people have the opportunity to see (OTS). There are reasonable targeting possibilities (eg inner-city versus rural site). A good site can cost over £100,000 a year to hire – and then there is the cost of the posters!

◆ **Magazines.** Highly targeted but circulation can be a problem. Unless distributed by subscription, is it really getting to the right people? Possibility of integrating advertising with editorial content, such as supplements and features – PR agencies will pay several hundred pounds a year for a service that highlights when a magazine is to run a special supplement or feature that might mention their client's new product.

Why advertise?

An advertisement can have various objectives. Here are just a few:

◆ Establish, maintain or enhance a company's overall image. An example might be ads for major petrol companies or banks.
◆ Increase demand for a type of product or service. For example, 'Tea. Best drink of the day' or 'Meat to live'.
◆ Increase sales of a particular product or service.
◆ Inform the public (of, for example, a home hazard or benefit entitlement).
◆ Tell customers about a brand-new product (a 'product launch campaign').

Who is advertising aimed at?

◆ Consumers (the end-user).
◆ Wholesalers or retail outlets.
◆ Official agencies, associations etc (eg lobbying).

The process of advertising

The process of advertising is a complicated subject that would need a complete book on its own just to scratch the surface. You could start by thinking about how advertising affects you, your family and friends.

Advertising is aimed at demographic classes:

- A Higher managerial, administrative or professional staff.
- B Intermediate managerial, administrative or professional staff.
- C1 Supervisory or clerical, junior manager, administrative or professional staff.
- C2 Skilled manual workers.
- D Semi-skilled and unskilled manual workers.
- E State pensioners, widows, casual or lowest-grade workers, etc.

When agencies talk of ads aimed at ABs, this means those with highest disposable income. Compare the ads in the papers and magazines you read, such as the *Sun* compared with *The Times*. (Incidentally, it was *The Times* that ran the first full-page nude ad.)

Read *Campaign*, *Marketing Week* etc and suggested books, and ask your local library if they have *Confessions of an Advertising Man* and *Ogilvy on Advertising* by David Ogilvy, one of the most famous figures in advertising. Ogilvy hated pomposity, believing that the business of advertising was to sell, and warned his staff that 'the consumer is not a moron – she is your wife'. He devised many famous campaigns such as 'Schhh… you know who'. To promote Hathaway shirts in the United States, he used a male model with a dashing eye patch. Everyone was soon talking about 'the man in the Hathaway shirt'.

Ogilvy made his first career mark selling Aga cookers. Realising that boarding-school headmasters would probably buy Agas when re-equipping schools, he wrote a sales letter in Latin to pander to their scholarship. He then wrote Aga's sales guide, which *Fortune Magazine* described as 'the best sales manual ever written'.

In 1948 he started a company that was to become one of the most successful advertising agencies in the world. His company helped British businesses trying to break into the US market and within three years he was regarded as one of the best copy-writers in the world.

Believing advertising should sell a product rather than simply amuse, he would choose one detail about a product for his ads. This produced one of the most famous adverts of all time: 'At 60 miles an hour, the loudest noise in this new Rolls-Royce comes from the electric clock.'

What kind of people work in advertising?

Many of the qualities for marketing apply equally in advertising. Staff move between these two areas during their careers. If you are an avid analyser of advertisements, approach tasks creatively and enjoy the gentle art of persuasion, advertising might be the profession for you.

Here is a senior account planner in a leading advertising agency talking.

> Each agency is different and demands different types of people. While a large agency might have a well-structured workforce with plenty of administrative support, a smaller company might expect to employ all-rounders who would be closely involved in most stages of a campaign. This is, without doubt, an industry where getting in is extremely difficult but where you can really get noticed once you arrive. The important thing is to get the right balance between working on your own initiative and learning from other people. At first, you know very little and, although experienced creatives and account handlers can get things right first time through instinct and expertise, it takes a lot of hard work to get to that stage.

For account managers, in particular, the importance of financial skills cannot be overestimated. In addition, advertising research work is extremely technical and a qualification in market research would be a distinct advantage. You have to be able to get on with clients; if you don't suffer fools gladly, keep your thoughts to yourself until you own the agency, like the legendary Colin Millward of Collett Dickenson Pearce. He paid his executives more than any other agency, then expected world-class work. To one account manager who reported that Harveys of Bristol Cream fame did not like their ad, he replied:

'Go back to Bristol and tell them we do ads and they make sherry.' But you have to be top of your profession before you can tell this to a client. If you want to keep your job.

Read some job advertisements to see what qualities employers are looking for – there are some examples in Chapter 9.

Case Study

***Ian** is senior account handler for a major advertising agency.*

I studied history at university, and hadn't much of an idea of what I wanted to do when I left. I had been heavily involved in music and drama, so I suppose I had demonstrated a creative streak of sorts. A few advertising agencies came round to recruit new graduates on the 'milk round'. I had interviews with several agencies and was lucky enough to be offered a job with this one – probably because they have an account where my interest in music could be useful.

Beginning as a graduate trainee, I spent a few weeks working in each department. This was part of the agency's excellent training programme, with discussions and seminars and practical project work, plus financial skills classes for those of us from arts backgrounds. While all this was extremely useful, I learnt quicker when I became part of an account group, helping out on tasks ranging from editorial work to sitting in on client presentations.

I was then given my own, small account to manage, although the account manager was always ready to give advice and to look at what I was doing. In this industry, clients are wary of being allocated to junior members of staff so, although they were not spending as much with us as the larger accounts, I had to ensure that they didn't feel neglected. It is quite often the smaller accounts that need more detailed work: they can be fussier about the administrative detail. I then moved on to one of our key accounts, working closely with a senior account manager. This felt like 'the deep end' and I learned more in the first month in this position than anywhere else.

The most difficult, and stimulating, part of an account handler's work is juggling all the different tasks and responsibilities, rearranging priorities when necessary and maintaining the right level of client liaison. The team working on this account work well together – you depend on each other so much for each stage of the planning, presentation and production. You are also inevitably working to tight deadlines much of the time, so the ability to pull together is critical.

Five years on, I am senior account manager in the same company, which is quite unusual – many people change jobs several times in the first few years, until they find an agency they feel comfortable in, or they might move in-house. I run one of our most important accounts, which is a major responsibility; no agency likes to lose an account, least of all one of its most important clients, so I have to ensure that we continue to supply high-quality analytical, creative and productive work. It's a competitive market – other agencies could be asked to pitch at any time and we could lose an account that had been with the company for ten years or more – it happens.

As you get higher in a company, you obviously do less of the administrative work and more of the corporate strategic planning and new account development. Ideally, I'd like to become a director of a small agency, perhaps outside London.

I'd recommend that anybody wanting to work in advertising tries to get on to one of the graduate trainee schemes run by an agency, and agencies tend to prefer graduates, although not necessarily with a business studies degree. If you have any contacts inside the industry, use them. They probably won't be able to offer you a job but you may get some holiday work or be able to talk to them about the sort of people they recruit.

Top Tips

And if you don't have very good academic qualifications, remember David Ogilvy didn't think ads had to be too clever. He said: 'People don't buy a new detergent because the manufacturer told a joke on TV… they buy it because it promises a benefit.'

Keep an open mind and don't believe everything you are told; over-hyped advertisements have been around for centuries. Dr Samuel Johnson wrote: 'Advertisements are now so numerous that they are very negligently perused, and it is therefore become necessary to gain attention by magnificence of promises.'

Another famous saying – attributed to many people (Lord Leverhulme and John Wanamaker amongst others) – was: 'I know that half my advertising budget is wasted, but I'm not sure which half.'

For the future

The ban on tobacco advertising has had an enormous effect on
the advertising and marketing industry, with companies diversifying into areas such as clothes, cosmetics and skin-care. Dunhill
now makes more money selling its branded luxury goods than
on cigarettes. Although 'duty free' sales suffered with the loss of
intra-EU duty free sales, the British Airports Authority have
managed to claw back lost sales by squeezing manufacturers'
margins, increasing advertising, and producing creative below-
the-line promotions that encouraged holidaymakers. Look out
for their 'buy before you fly' campaigns.

4 Public relations

What is public relations?

The Institute of Public Relations (IPR) says: 'Public relations is the deliberate, planned and sustained effort to establish and maintain mutual understanding between an organisation and its public.'

Although it may be difficult to evaluate or quantify the success of PR activity, it is obvious when it isn't done well. Some of the best examples of successful and important PR activity have been in recent years, when communication of information about major transport or financial disasters, for example, has been handled well by PR experts.

Unfortunately, examples of unsuccessful PR are easy to spot, when an organisation is heavily criticised in the press and does little to protect its image.

Once PR was sometimes seen as second in importance to advertising, but an article in *PR Week* says evidence of the improved position of PR can be found in the recent launches such as Apple's iMac computer, given a PR launch four months before the ad campaign kicked in. Shell put their PR agency in the lead role in its first global communications campaign, handing the task to Fishburn Hedges. Volkswagen and Gillette also chose PR to lead recent launches.

As with advertising, PR professionals can work in-house, for agencies or freelance. One of the most striking aspects of PR is the breadth of activities it covers. Nearly every organisation wants to influence the way in which it is seen by individuals and groups. Its 'public' can include local communities, share-holders, employees within the organisation, the retail trade, etc.

The public may question what good PR can achieve. But as Kate Nicholas, editor of *PR Week* magazine, points out, without PR 'companies would be left free to pollute and exploit the environments they operate in, unhampered by PR-savvy pressure groups... and private shareholders and pensioners would know little about the companies in which their futures are invested'.

The process of PR

PR could involve working directly for a company, providing information about that company to the general public and the media. Or it could be working for an agency specialising in handling PR for client companies.

Companies and organisations, from government to manufacturers, need to keep in contact with the public. This is done by brochures, leaflets, videos, CD ROMs, Web pages, press releases, exhibitions, conferences etc.

The work can be glamorous – PR executives often meet clients in exciting places. The downside is long hours and travelling – often arriving home after midnight and having to be on the road again early next morning.

Many journalists look longingly at PR companies and wonder if it is worthwhile swapping over to theoretically lusher fields. However, in PR you are paid to promote your clients' products, rather than write about them, which can stifle creativity. Sometimes staff move over from advertising or marketing into PR because they have specialised knowledge. Richard Lane is an example. Richard worked for the *Independent* newspaper in the advertising and marketing departments, then became Press Officer for the RNIB. He was Media Relations Manager for Guide Dogs for the Blind and he and Norton, his guide dog, were familiar figures at press conferences. Currently he is involved as a trustee.

Most PR companies look for graduates and almost any degree will be useful. If you have experience in cosmetics, motor trade, retailing, etc, you can often build on this when looking for a job.

There are some university courses in PR and parts of CAM courses that offer useful work experience, but dealing with the public (press, shareholders, local community etc) is a combination of inherent skill and acquired expertise. There is no substitute for experience, and this is what employers look for. There is a large amount of in-house training for any facet of PR work, from marketing to conference administration; CAM, ACE and the IPR have useful training courses.

PR work demands close liaison with all the marketing staff within an organisation, with a clear idea of objectives and plans. An agency will appoint account managers for each client and, as with an advertising agency, the account manager carries out communications activities for the client within an agreed budget. Much PR work involves communicating with the press, so an understanding of how journalists work is important.

A PR manager for a building society, for example, would ensure that the press, shareholders, government and important groups are kept constantly updated with the society's activities – particularly its successes. If any unfavourable news was on the cards – either about that building society or societies as a whole – the PR manager needs to pre-empt it, sending press or news releases or holding press conferences to communicate the society's stand on the issue.

Another example of the importance of PR is the part played in communicating information after a disaster, where a system is in place for dealing with emergency press calls – and those of families – within minutes of the event. This has been called 'crisis PR', and although it does not alleviate suffering, it can certainly restore confidence in the organisation much faster than if it were to shrug off the public in its hour of need. Organisations have become much more aware of this fact over the past decade and many have very sophisticated emergency systems in place. The same is true when a product has been contaminated or is dangerous – through either mechanical error or criminal activity – and the organisation needs to communicate as quickly as possible to all its distribution channels (shops, restaurants, bars etc) in precisely the right way to avoid disaster, panic or loss of confidence in the product.

What kind of people work in PR?

Ex-journalists understand what will interest the press and how to present a story in the most effective way to get media coverage (or to avoid getting negative coverage). The ability to write well is essential, picking out salient facts and expressing them in the most succinct and eye-catching way. Look at recruitment advertisements (see Chapter 9) to see what recruiters look for.

If you work in an agency, communication with clients is all-important. A good relationship is vital – and can be difficult if the client seems unreasonably demanding. It is important that your role is clearly established from the beginning and that both parties realise PR activity could be endless: there is no end to the work you could do!

First jobs will probably be as a junior in an agency or an information assistant for a local authority, tourist board, etc. Work experience or journalism gets your foot in the door; the National Council for the Training of Journalists (NCTJ) say their trainees 'all get fixed up with a job on local newspapers'. CAM and IPR can also advise on courses.

PR Week lists the top ten UK agencies by 'billings' (the amount they bill, or turnover) and the number of people employed:

- Weber Shandwick (419 employees);
- Citigate Dewe Rogerson (308 employees);
- Bell Pottinger Communications (300 employees);
- Hill and Knowlton (368 employees);
- Countrywide Porter Novelli (264 employees);
- BSMG Worldwide (UK) (223 employees);
- Burston-Marsteller (194 employees);
- GCI/APCO UK (231 employees);
- Financial Dynamics (146 employees);
- Good Relations (156 employees).

The names usually come from surnames of founders. You can look up their clients in the *Advertisers Annual*.

Case Study

Donna *is PR executive for a financial services company.*

At university I studied French and thought I wanted to be a translator. However, I took a temporary job in a PR agency and the more I found out about it, the more I wanted to work in the industry permanently. The temporary job lasted for six months, so I was able to observe what went on and even make some contacts that have been useful in my present position. I spotted an advertisement in the paper for a junior in a small agency: no experience needed, but patience, enthusiasm and excellent communication skills.

It might sound odd, but I had done quite a bit of acting at college and I am sure this helped me. You spend a lot of time convincing people about things: the more professional your approach, the more persuasive you can be. That first job involved updating press lists, organising printing and generally supporting the account managers, who always seemed desperately busy.

The agency then promoted me assistant to an account manager. This was my first real 'break' and I worked extremely hard to get it right, often spending long hours in the office before a major presentation to the client or a press launch. In PR, the type of work you do depends very much on your client. If it is an FMCG manufacturer, you may be running promotions in magazines, liaising closely with an advertising agency on the launch of a new product, organising countrywide theme days – anything that encourages understanding between the company and its public. Or you could be working for a local authority, communicating its activities, aims and successes to the community.

I studied for the Chartered Institute of Marketing's Diploma in Marketing in the evenings, and although PR was only a part of the Communications course, it was useful to work on how it fitted in with the rest of the marketing mix.

After four years, I decided I would like to move in-house, working for a company on their PR, so I moved here and began working in financial PR. It is a highly competitive field. We do have a PR agency which carries out a great deal of our specialist work, and one of my jobs is liaison between the agency and ourselves. The financial services industry has had a difficult time in recent years and one of our tasks has been to restore confidence in our services and our commitment to the service of our customers. This is precisely where PR is most important – and most stimulating. It's hard work, though – and anyone looking for a nine-to-five job shouldn't consider PR.

In the consumer skincare industry you work closely with in-store demonstrators (see Chapter 2) to find out what the public say and want. PR varies from events with supermodels to discreet PR used to publicise a luxury brand. PR for luxury skincare products is often by word of mouth between customers; it is your job to harness this goodwill, and build on it. Companies such as La Prairie, for example, inform their in-store demonstrators when new products are coming from Switzerland; the demonstrators then tell customers – and stand back whilst customers create their own sales rush. The same thing happens with luxury goods, especially Chanel and Kelly handbags.

PR can mean keeping information out of the press. For instance, the French skin-care company Sisley are very careful about where they publicise their products. Sisley's PR department is there to see that their brand promotion is handled carefully and reaches customers who understand the benefits of its plant-based skin-care, rather than diluting the message with articles on 'the most expensive', which won't create the impression of well-researched products that Sisley wish to put over.

A good PR should react quickly when phoned by journalists. Take this example. Reading an article about protecting skin from today's environmental pollutants, Trudi, a freelance journalist, thought this was a good topic for her monthly column on skincare for a national magazine. She had previously written about PX Prescriptives' wrinkle-control oil and thought it very good, so she called Anna in the Press Office to ask for comments. Anna said they were just about to launch 'Timeproof', a broad-spectrum moisturiser that shielded against photo-ageing, helped boost the skin's defences against damaging environmental effects, and was a moisturiser. It had a USP: not only did it have SPF 15 sun protection, but Anna said it was formulated to protect against damage caused by reflected light from PC screens. 'I'll send you some.' An hour later, a courier arrived on Trudi's doorstep with the product. 'I was intrigued, tried it, liked it and thanks to Anna got some intelligent quotes from Jules Zecchino, Prescriptives' Executive Director of Research and Development: "In times of stress the body diverts blood away from skin and pumps it to organs such as heart and lungs that are more vital for survival", so it is essential to help your face and skin protect themselves from environmental damage. Good stuff. It made an interesting hook.' And she had written and filed the article by the time rival companies' products arrived days later.

Press conferences

Organising press conferences is an important part of PR work. Trudi goes to many:

> and I despair at times. They are often held in low-ceilinged rooms, so those at the back can't see the platform. The PR company staff have been drafted in for the day, so don't know what the clients look like when I ask to meet an executive. Champagne is served but no soft drinks (some of us have to work afterwards) and the glossy bimbos from the agency seem to think that we will be grateful for a press release, then go away and write up the company message. Fat chance.
>
> I did go to an excellent press conference the other day, organised by Brighter PR for Carlson, a leading American travel and tourism group. The invitation arrived with short biographies of the executives who would be present, including Chief Executive Marilyn Carlson Nelson, and a fax-back form that we could tick stating whom we wanted to interview. Arriving at the Radisson Hampshire Hotel, a smart PR met us, offered excellent coffee and biscuits and introduced us to Mrs Nelson herself. This was refreshing; so often at British press conferences the executives don't bother to turn up until it is time to sit on the platform; they want the honour without working for the glory. Carlson gave us no gimmicks, just solid quotable facts and figures from everyone who spoke. We learnt about the company's major shareholding in Thomas Cook, the new Radisson all-suite luxury cruise liners and how the company aimed to bring 350,000 US travellers to Europe in the next year. I came away with a file of quotes to be included in forthcoming articles and some solid background information that will be useful in the future.

Conferences and events

PR can also involve events such as a royal visit, a 'reveal' (when a new car is announced and shown off to the press), a company's sales conference etc. Sometimes these are organised in-house, but generally a professional conference organiser (PCO) or event organiser will work freelance for a company's press department or for their PR agency.

A reveal can involve transporting several hundred people to an exotic location. The destination is secret, so dealers and press get to see the car before the public. The location has to be interesting and/or exotic, encouraging dealers to take time away from their showrooms and journalists to make time in a busy schedule.

Ford organised a reveal in Malta. When their specially chartered planes landed, dealers could look out of the windows to see the new cars driving along the runway. Whilst they were being whisked off to a celebration lunch, their luggage was taken straight to their hotel rooms. Whilst dealers tried out the new car, their spouses went on shopping trips. That evening there was a grand fireworks display and next morning the hard sell started, with salesmen talking delivery dates and order numbers. A very expensive exercise, but cost-effective. Happy dealers are much more optimistic about the numbers of cars they propose to sell.

For those who weren't able to make it to Malta, the PR department organised another reveal held in a giant aircraft hangar in the Midlands. The production company packaged the set as a giant parcel, which burst open revealing the car floating on a cloud of dry ice. There was an all-singing, all-dancing show, compèred by a well-known comedian, who hyped everyone up so they felt part of a glamorous occasion. Afterwards, the salesforce moved in to discuss sales.

Another type of event is the incentive conference, and PR is often involved with exhibitions. See Chapter 6 for more information.

Basic qualifications

For basic qualifications in this sector, there is a GNVQ administered by City and Guilds, an NVQ for the events industry (contact the Events Sector Industry Training Organisation (ESITO)), and coming on-stream a new vocational qualification run by Pan Aviation Services. The airline industry is desperate for better-qualified entrants, but when it had difficulty recruiting these, MD Pat Egan went to employers, asked what they wanted, and developed a Vocational Qualification for Cabin Crew. This was so successful that over 400 students from the first year were taken on by airlines.

This is what should have happened with GNVQs, but instead colleges picked up courses that got more students, rather than asking the industry what it wanted. If the Conference and Events VQ gets the same response as the Cabin Crew VQ, it will prove that in education market forces also dictate what is offered. See Chapter 8 for more information.

Books

The industry 'bibles' are *Hollis UK Press and PR Annual*, which lists just about every PR consultancy and contacts for companies that handle PR in-house; and *Willings Press Guide*, which gives details of over 20,000 media titles in the UK. There is also an international edition with 30,000 contacts worldwide.

For an insider's guide to PR, read Annie Gurton's book *Press Here!*. Witty and informative, she doesn't pull punches, especially when writing about inept PR. I am sure you would never make the same mistakes!

Direct marketing

What is direct marketing?

Professor Derek Holder, Managing Director of the Institute of Direct Marketing, the profession's leading research, training and education body in the UK, describes direct marketing as 'the fusion of creative thinking with customer knowledge and the latest technologies to generate customised communications and business solutions'.

In 2001 expenditure on direct marketing in the UK topped £10 billion. Around 50,000 people work in direct marketing in the UK, and approximately 5,000 jobs are created each year (L Fields (1997) You can't get the staff these days, *Marketing*, 28 August, pp 14–15).

The key distinction between direct marketing and other forms of marketing is that the results of direct marketing are measurable. For example, during a one-off telemarketing campaign the exact number of calls, responses and sales can be determined and the cost of the campaign weighed against the income generated. The customer database can be updated by recording the response of every individual. These new data can then be analysed to profile the characteristics of customers most likely to purchase and then used to identify the best prospects already on the customer database. Alternatively, it can provide an outline of preferred prospects if the marketing organisation is going to rent or buy a list from a third party supplier. In short, direct marketing is all about using data to create products and offers through a one-to-one relationship between the individual consumer and the brand.

Direct marketers communicate using a mix of media such as e-mail, postal mail, press advertising, SMS (short messaging service) messages, telemarketing, direct response television and the Internet to build brands, influence consumer opinion and increase sales.

How does it work?

Think of direct marketing as a relationship between:

- ◆ the client – the company or individual that wishes to use direct marketing;
- ◆ the agency – the body recruited to provide the direct marketing service;
- ◆ the supplier – the specialist provider of marketing services (print, telemarketing, mail houses, etc).

Clients can come from almost any business background – from charities to airlines and financial services. Many larger clients will have their own marketing department who brief agencies for particular brands or campaigns and may carry out a portion of the marketing activity themselves. The structure varies from organisation to organisation.

Agencies come in all shapes and sizes; some specialise purely in direct marketing, while others offer direct marketing as part and parcel of a wider marketing communications portfolio. Whichever category an agency falls into, it is likely to be structured in a similar way, usually comprising four key groups. These are:

- ◆ account management – often the central focus of the agency, as this is the interface with the client;
- ◆ creative – where a client's brief becomes an idea and ultimately the communication to the customer;
- ◆ production – where the promotion is put together; and
- ◆ planning – both account and data planning.

Suppliers provide the support services that make direct marketing possible, and it is usually the job of the agency to appoint and manage the relationship with the supplier. There is a wealth of suppliers to the profession but among the most frequently used are mailing houses, fulfilment, telemarketing, data processing, laser printing, list profiling and media buying.

Who uses direct marketing?

Financial services are big users: Direct Line and Goldfish credit cards were unheard of a few years back, until they used direct marketing. Established brands like Marks and Spencer have also jumped on the financial services bandwagon using direct marketing to carry their message, with phenomenal success.

Furthermore, a number of big businesses have applied the principles of direct marketing to improve customer relations, to hold on to existing customers in today's more competitive environment, and also to increase sales. Tesco's Clubcard is an obvious example.

──────────────── **Case Study** ────────────────

How does direct marketing work? Example 1

The music industry is unpredictable. Bands with youth appeal in particular have a pretty short shelf life. And even with regard to artists that are successful over a longer-term, few labels really know the people that comprise their markets since most sales are made through third party channels like High Street stores and Web sites.

It was a problem familiar to record label BMG – home of Westlife, Natalie Imbruglia and Will Young – and they came up with the idea of using direct marketing to provide the solution. In Christmas 2001, when Westlife and Natalie Imbruglia both had new albums coming out, BMG was presented with the opportunity to promote each album with a direct marketing campaign. This was conceived not only to promote the artists and albums themselves but also to capture data on the record buyers and re-establish loyalty to BMG.

Because of competition from Internet downloads and pirate copies of albums, BMG had to come up with something more than the albums themselves. The solution was to reach fans by offering them something that no one else could. Steve Hanney, head of direct marketing for BMG Europe, decided to offer fans an exclusive song or video online – but only if they could prove they had bought a genuine copy of the respective artist's last album.

Imbruglia recorded an exclusive song and Westlife recorded some exclusive interviews, which were edited with never before seen concert footage. BMG then got to work on the mailer and the corresponding part of each artist's Web site for the pan-European campaign.

Hanney then went through the painstaking task of compiling the lists by first looking at the types of people stored on BMG's own database and then matching their profiles with prospects from third party suppliers' lists. And to ensure that everything was above board, 20 lawyers were brought in to make certain that everything complied with data protection legislation.

In October 2001, 10 million people across Europe were mailed, telling them that if they bought one of the albums they could have the exclusive track or footage from the artist's respective Web site. The campaign was a phenomenal success in its own right, with the Westlife album going straight to number one. Spin-off projects from it include the launch of an online Westlife fan club.

Most importantly, BMG have captured a vast amount of data on Europe's record-buying public for use in more targeted artist-specific promotions.

Source: Marketing Direct, April 2002

Case Study

How does direct marketing work? Example 2

YouthNet (thesite.org) was created by the broadcaster Martyn Lewis in 1994 as a resource from which 16- to 24-year-olds could seek high-quality, factual advice about such subjects as drugs, sex, careers and relationships. From June 2001 thesite.org wanted to drive its user base up by 500 per cent over a 12-month period.

To achieve this, new media marketing agency Digital Outlook designed the 'animal sex quiz' to appeal to the core audience. In essence, the quiz asks a series of simple questions to determine what kind of 'animal' participants are when playing the mating game.

Online marketing activity specifically chosen to act as a catalyst for viral effect was employed, by targeting Web sites proven to attract 16- to

24-year-olds to stimulate the viral effect thesite.org was seeking. Some 'guerrilla marketing activity' was undertaken – that is, going into specific online communities as well-known and trusted personas and discussing what results they had received. Digital Outlook also targeted e-mail lists that reflected the target audience, including some known to include opinion formers who would be more likely to pass on the quiz and/or talk about it.

Marketing activity lasted approximately five weeks, after which no additional marketing was undertaken. All subsequent activity has resulted from the viral effect taking hold. Where possible, the spread of the quiz was monitored and found to result largely from postings on Internet discussion boards, with each thread generating up to 150 responses – demonstrating the interest levels generated by the quiz content.

To date there have been over 329,000 plays of the quiz, and this number is currently rising at approximately 10,000 plays a day. On a cost per user basis this works out at approximately 4p per user and it is worth noting that the game-play peak has not yet been reached, and so the final cost per user is likely to be significantly lower.

As a result of this increased activity, thesite.org has increased its weekly unique users from a figure around 12,000 in June 2001 to a new high of 132,000. Monthly page impressions had also increased to 2.1 million by March 2002.

What kinds of people work in direct marketing?

BMG and thesite.org are just two examples; there are many other users of and uses for direct marketing. For that reason, direct marketing involves people from all academic disciplines and backgrounds.

Those who are good with numbers will enjoy the statistical analysis of the research stages and examining the responses to questionnaires. Candidates with good writing skills will excel in writing tailored copy persuading people from all kinds of backgrounds either to switch brand or remain loyal, as the case may be. Creative thinkers will enjoy planning campaigns to deliver objectives on time and on budget to a clearly specified audience. Good communicators will enjoy research through focus groups and designing scripts for telemarketing activities with prepared replies for the many possible responses to calls.

Overall, effective networkers and those with good communication skills, both written and oral, are most likely to succeed in direct marketing because it is first and foremost a people profession.

For more information about careers in direct marketing, contact the Institute of Direct Marketing on 020 8614 0272 or visit the Web site at www.think-direct.com.

Call centres

Although classified as 'below the line' (see Chapter 6), these come under direct marketing and are one of the largest employers of marketing staff. Many ads on TV and in newspapers give an 0800 number to call for information, where callers are usually routed through to a call centre. This is telemarketing: using the telephone as a marketing tool.

In a call centre there are rows of people with headsets sitting in front of a screen. Their job is to get your name and address so another centre can send out literature – but often not to answer complicated queries, as this takes more time. Working in a centre can be stressful – staff are often on performance-related bonuses.

Call centres know no borders. Say someone living in Spain wants to book an airline ticket to the United States. He or she calls Delta and is seamlessly patched (routed) through to London, where a Spanish-speaking person takes his or her booking. However, this system doesn't work as well for IT companies such as Hewlett-Packard. Call its helpline from the UK and you go through to the Netherlands. Although call centre staff speak English, they may not actually think on the same wavelength.

However, call centres are here to stay. Staff may not stay very long, so there is always a job if you want an insight into another side of the industry. The training is extremely effective and could provide a fast introduction into marketing and selling techniques.

Below-the-line

What is below-the-line advertising?

'Above the line' was originally used to describe TV, radio, poster and print advertisements; in other words, any way of promoting to the public what is read or seen on paper, or heard or viewed on radio or TV. This was probably from the 'line' used to distinguish between advertising that paid commission and that 'below the line' that didn't.

Below-the-line advertising covers the vast 'indirect' promotion and marketing industry. The name is an elastic term, describing any way of promoting a product that doesn't fall into the above paragraph; it includes leaflet distribution, direct mail, point-of-sale promotions, exhibitions, incentives, etc.

Below-the-line is an expanding section of the industry; the Institute of Sales Promotion says that the market for direct mail, competitions, instant wins, discounts, Web site offers, etc is worth about £10 billion a year. When a leaflet falls through the letter-box or you attend an exhibition, you are a 'user' of this section of the industry.

Exhibitions have a high profile, with a turnover estimated at over £850 million a year.

Field marketing covers selling, merchandising, sampling and demonstrating a product to the consumer. Stop at a petrol station because you are collecting their glasses or take the advice of the nice promotions person in the supermarket who urges you to buy their soap powder because you will have a chance to win a holiday to Florida – again, you have been persuaded by below-the-line advertising.

Incentive conferences

If your local store has a big promotion publicising a line of branded goods, this is probably because the manufacturer is running an incentive promotion offering something special – usually a holiday, under the guise of an incentive conference – to salespeople who increase sales. Travel companies that specialise in handling these incentives have turnovers in the high millions.

Companies often use incentives as part of their promotions strategy, but it isn't just a case of offering a holiday to an exotic destination. A well-run incentive is 'self-liquidating' – extra sales pay for the incentive holidays and give the company a higher profit. There is usually a conference incorporated into the holiday, so the company can spread the word for the future.

Leaflet distribution

Leaflets can be handed to you in the street, left under a car windscreen wiper or dropped through your letter-box. Although conversion rates are small, this can be an inexpensive way to promote. Many promotions companies need staff to distribute leaflets and can offer students part-time work.

Case Study

Susan has worked as a senior account manager in a sales promotion agency for four years, progressing from account executive to senior account manager, responsible for a major drinks account. The sales promotion agency is part of a major international advertising organisation.

Sales promotion is often used by consumer companies looking for a specific, immediate response – for instance, to increase sales over a short period by running a campaign offering 'two for the price of one' or encouraging the collection of tokens to be swapped for a free gift (a technique frequently used by a company looking to take market share from a competing brand).

Usually a sales promotion is undertaken by an external agency rather than in-house, as few companies want to pay for permanent sales promotion staff when they use it on a project-by-project basis. Even for those fast-moving consumer goods manufacturers using sales promotion regularly, an agency is usually a more effective way of operating.

I have a team of three working with me on this account. The agency is kept on a retainer by the client company and we are then given the budget, which may be several million pounds, at the beginning of each year. The client briefs me on its objectives that year, which could be to increase wholesaler support of a particular brand, develop business through the multiples or improve customer brand loyalty. I devise and cost the sales promotion strategy to achieve these objectives and present this to the client at my most important meeting each year. To pitch, I also need the skills of the creative department, who create slogans and copy, and the design department, who will provide mock-ups of the on-pack offers or direct mailshots.

A significant part of my time is spent doing the costings for the promotion: we have to make absolutely sure that we have planned for the right number of responses, have access to enough stock of the incentive gift and will not receive so many responses that the cost of the promotion will outweigh any benefit in increased sales! Sales promotion can involve off-the-page 'sponsored' promotions in magazines and on-cover free offers (sachets of shampoo, free floppy disks, etc), so we deal with the media, booking space and organising for the fulfilment of free offers.

The company runs a trainee scheme: three new recruits are taken on each year who spend the first six months in various departments, including creative, design, planning and accounting. They are then assigned as 'junior account executives' to a particular account, learning about the whole integrated sales promotion process. I'd recommend that anybody interested in sales promotion contacts all the agencies they can find to see whether they run a trainee scheme. (The major companies are listed in the *Advertisers Annual – The Blue Book*.) If not, it might be better to join a general marketing department and try to move across.

Below-the-line in practice

Let's look how Susan's company would promote a new product. A major manufacturer of blenders has carried out market research, which concludes that there is a market for an inexpensive 'no-frills' blender. It has developed 'Fruit Wizzer' –

a low-cost juicer that turns fruit and vegetables into juice and smoothies. Analysing market research makes Susan's company believe they will be able to make a profit, provided they run a campaign to tell the public about the machine. Susan's team decide the best way of promoting the product to the general public is to run in-store promotions nationally in supermarkets, shopping malls and department stores.

In-store promotions

Sites have been selected at 200 major outlets around Britain where demonstrators can promote and sell Fruit Wizzer. Collapsible stands are being designed and built to form a focal point for the promotion. Susan asks a company to design an inexpensive but eye-catching uniform for the demonstrators; she wants a white suit giving an impression of purity – until someone points out that these will soon get stained. So they settle on a large plastic apron with fruit screen-printed on.

A field merchandising company is asked to provide a team of five smart, presentable field promotions executives (FPEs). They have to be able to drive a car, erect the simple stand, take charge of demonstrators, liaise with the stores and be available for five consecutive weeks. Each FPE has a section of the country to supervise and will have to ensure samples and supplies are available.

Every Tuesday the FPE meets locally booked demonstrators and briefs them, and meets the managers and confirms they have allocated Fruit Wizzer a prime site for the demonstration; this is repeated in all local stores featuring the Fruit Wizzer demonstration. From Wednesday to Friday the FPE might organise a demonstration for the Women's Institute or be present at a photo-call with the local newspaper where a Fruit Wizzer is being given away as a prize for a competition, then go round the stores keeping the demonstrators' spirits up and making sure they have enough supplies. There are sales reports to write and returns to fill out and send in.

Saturday is the busiest day: after the stores close the FPE has to go round collecting (and probably dismantling) the stands. The demonstrators are supposed to do this but when you have been on your feet for five solid days you just want to get home. Sunday is for completing paperwork, before setting off on Monday to drive to the next area of the UK selected for the promotion and deliver the stands, in the meantime accounting for aprons, samples, cloths and cleaners.

Like FPEs, demonstrators are freelances. One week they can be working at the local store promoting the Fruit Wizzer, the next week welcoming visitors to an exhibition stand.

Top Tips

If you are looking for work experience, before Christmas there is a tremendous amount of work for freelances to demonstrate perfumes and cosmetic gifts. Most cosmetics companies that have outlets in stores around Britain will take on temporary staff to handle the Christmas rush. Staff get commission on sales which can be profitable – but you have to stay selling right up until Christmas! Ask at your nearest department store.

Exhibitions

There are two kinds of exhibitions: public and trade.

Public exhibitions are open to everyone who pays for a ticket. Exhibitors are there to sell and/or inform visitors about their product.

Trade exhibitions are only open to invited guests and/or those working in the relevant industry. At trade exhibitions it is visitor quality, not quantity, that counts. Stand managers want their staff to talk to people who are actually prepared to buy their product, not just look.

Hotels and conference venues spend a large proportion of their promotions budgets at exhibitions. These are seen as being the most effective venue to sell to large buyers such as tour operators and conference organisers.

Exhibition organiser Ray Bloom realised that if he could offer these buyers 'on a plate' to exhibitors such as hoteliers, conference venues, etc, they would sign up for stand space at his European Incentive Business Travel and Meetings Exhibition (EIBTM) in Geneva. He hit upon the idea of inviting these people as guests; EIBTM pays their travel and hotel costs, amortising these across stand charges.

The idea took off and the exhibition has grown until it now has exhibitors from Abu Dhabi to Zimbabwe. There are over 5,000 visitors; over half hosted by the organisers; the rest living locally. Representatives from incentive and conference organisers in the pharmaceutical, chemical, finance, banking, food, electronics and other industries look for venues and new ideas for their clients. EIBTM fills Palexpo Exhibition Centre and the exhibition is now a firm fixture in the diaries of top travel professionals.

Since EIBTM started the trend, other exhibitions and meetings now offer 'hosted buyer' schemes to encourage exhibitors to take stand space.

Sponsorship

Every time you see Cutty Sark Tall Ships Race, Whitbread Gold Cup, Mitsubishi Badminton Horse Trials, Veuve Clicquot Polo Gold Cup, etc mentioned in the press, you are reading a subtle promotion for a company.

Most major events can no longer survive just on ticket sales and entrance fees. So they sell the right to rename the event after the sponsoring company. For over 30 years Cutty Sark Whisky has sponsored the Tall Ships race, gaining publicity in return. The synergy is there: the whisky was named after the graceful old sailing ships and the sailing ship symbol on bottle labels is reproduced on every poster mentioning the race.

Not every port visited by the race is in a country that sells Cutty Sark – so it's win some, lose some. However, square-rigged ships draw up to 2 million visitors in each port they visit; multiply this by the number of times Cutty Sark Tall Ships is written in newspapers and talked about on the radio and TV, and you can see how sponsorship can be a powerful medium in promoting a brand name.

There are many opportunities to work in this sector, for:

◆ agencies with clients involved in sponsorship;
◆ companies dealing with sponsorship;
◆ events offices in the lead–up to the event.

Corporate hospitality events

A corporate hospitality event involves a company deciding to invite their best clients to a special event to say 'thank you' for their custom and encourage customer loyalty. As the company is 'on show', the occasion has to provide the best available food and entertainment. Guests could be invited to an event where it is difficult to get tickets, such as Wimbledon, Silverstone, Cowdray Gold Cup; or to something extra special that would be difficult to organise themselves. Events can be held at a specially hired stately home or an interesting venue not normally opened to the public.

Generally the Press Office of a company, or their PR agency, is in charge of the day, although they may go to an outside agency, usually a member of the Corporate Events Association, to provide the ideas and organisation. CEA members have to abide by a strict code of conduct, taking in health and safety requirements, and insure the guests and the event for a large sum.

Organising an event

Let's continue the example we were looking at earlier.

Sales of Fruit Wizzer have exceeded all expectations. The MD wants to thank dealers and subtly ensure that they don't decide to stock competing products. It is October, and he calls in Penny from the PR department to tell her that he wants her to organise a 'thank you' day. The budget is £300 per person and he thinks he will invite about 40 dealers. 'Go away and plan a really good day out,' he tells her.

Easier said than done. It will take time to organise, and

Christmas is on the horizon. Everything is booked up, so Penny wonders about a post-Christmas day out. And should she make it a mystery tour? She has several ideas she picked up at CONFEX (the Conference Industry Exhibition) and one, from Sam's company, was organising mystery days out with a twist. The MD likes the idea. He and his wife have just come back from a weekend in Lille. Mrs MD loved the city, so he suggests a mystery tour to Lille. (This MD's wife has a great deal of clout!)

Sam's first suggestion is cut down on the number of guests – two per employee-host is about right – and invite their partners. Business executives on their own tend to cancel at the last minute; if their partners are coming they seldom cancel.

Sam phones Vera Dupuis, the Tourism Officer of Lille, who arranges a familiarisation trip to show what Lille can offer. Penny likes the idea of travelling by Eurostar. When they arrive, Vera is brimming with ideas, whisking them off to walk through the town. As they walk around, Sam comes up with the idea that it would be fun to have a treasure hunt, using the shop that sells over 100 varieties of tea, a charming little museum with unusual exhibits and the Musée des Beaux Arts, where there are huge relief maps used to train spies in the last century.

At each stop Sam and Penny pick up cards and samples and Vera introduces them to the manageress of the Hermès shop. They arrange for her to give a special demonstration of different ways to tie their scarves. Sam and Penny would like to give one to each female guest, but they cost £165! So Vera suggests a numbered ticket with a prize of a scarf or silk tie.

Vera takes them to lunch at L'Ecume des Mers, buzzing with locals and built so cleverly that there will be room for their group to have a private balcony but still feel part of the restaurant. Food is very important, so they spend time on planning the menu around the house speciality of giant seafood platters. For vegetarians, those with an allergy or who don't like seafood, there will be a choice from the menu.

In the next few weeks there is a huge amount of planning if Sam's company are to ensure everything goes smoothly and keep the dealers and their partners happy.

Penny wants to give the guests a sightseeing trip after lunch but Sam and Vera dissuade her. A real 'French' gourmet meal will take almost all the afternoon and the company should have time to subtly talk over sales with their guests. Afterwards there will just be time for the visit to Hermès, before catching the Eurostar back – with champagne and canapés in case anyone is still hungry!

When they return Sam and Penny give a presentation, backed up with photos, to the MD and the marketing and sales directors. 'I think you have cracked this – you've made me enthusiastic,' says the marketing manager, 'but you must ask our insurers to make sure we cover every eventuality – including cancellation.' Penny added that if it rains she has an umbrella for each couple printed with the company logo.

Invitations go out inviting guests and partners for a mystery day out – and telling them not to forget their passports. Next week, those that have accepted are sent a little box containing delicious wafers. Inside the box there is a teaser: 'These are the favourite wafers of a famous general – present this card at the shop and you will be given a box to take home.' Penny knows that those that haven't replied will be hurrying to send their acceptances. Two weeks later out goes a little sample bottle of perfume and another voucher that says: 'Find me and choose a bottle from my shop.'

On the day of the trip, everyone is at the Eurostar Terminal waiting to board the train with its reserved carriage and champagne breakfast. On the train Sam and Penny tell everyone they are going to Lille and hand out a treasure hunt map. At each spot marked on the map there is a little prize to be collected.

Vera has arranged taxi vouchers. Each dealer and his or her partner is accompanied by a company representative – and off they go. Everyone has been given a card with the name, address and telephone number of the restaurant and instructed that they have to be there by 1.30. Everyone arrives at the restaurant clutching their spoils. They are all in a good mood, which gets better during lunch, but Sam and Penny know that they are still on duty to make sure everything goes well.

When lunch is almost over, Penny slips out to alert Hermès, where the group goes after lunch.

All in all, a very tired but happy bunch returns to Waterloo. The MD gets a letter or phone call from every one of the guests, many of them enclosing more orders, so he is satisfied.

Now Sam and Penny have to think where to go next year!

Working from home

Millions, from PR people to Web page designers, work from a home base, with numbers rising. It can seem a good idea but there are disadvantages: you are on your own, so you have to motivate yourself; and you have to sort out IT problems – no longer is there a colleague who can tell you how to work the latest gizmo, and professional help is expensive.

However, it can be rewarding, and many people have set up in business from their homes and found satisfaction building up their own company.

The Internet

Increasingly, people use the Internet to book flights and holidays and to buy clothes, books, etc. They use e-mail to keep in touch with friends and family, and in business to such an extent that some companies are suffering e-mail overload. There is work for those who understand Internet marketing and the dynamics of Web sites.

If this is new to you, a few brief words about the Internet may help. The Internet is accessed through a modem slotted into your computer. Internet access is cheap: around £15 a month for unlimited (but slow) access, or roughly double for faster broadband access. Once you are signed up, it doesn't cost any more even if you use the service 24 hours a day. Internet access can save money in unexpected ways: don't pay for

Directory Enquiries, go instead to a search engine like www.google.com, tap in the name of the company – and generally their contact details come up in seconds. All for free!

In theory, the Internet has opened up unimaginable resources of information, but often there is no way of checking if it is accurate. Recently a story in the *Daily Mail* said Lindberg was the first person to fly the Atlantic. Well, he was American; most Americans don't know that Alcock and Brown were actually the first, and the journalist admitted he had found his information on a US Internet site. No one has yet found a better way of checking than using reference books in the library – you have been warned!

E-mail opened up an inexpensive way of communicating, but unfortunately there are signs that people are now tending to ignore it, as they did earlier with faxes. Companies are now having a day when employees are not allowed to use the Net, but have to communicate via the telephone, and journalists needing information quickly have gone back to using the phone.

Marketing on the Internet

Although Microsoft president Steve Ballmer says the boom in electronic commerce has barely even started (he would, wouldn't he?), analysts say the take-up of e-commerce hasn't been as rapid as one would imagine. Consumer fears over giving out credit card details are one reason. Another is that Web site design is not as user-friendly as it could be. Microsoft's Web site is a case in point.

Common wisdom is that currently very few companies are making money marketing on the Internet, except those offering 'adult' products. There have been spectacular failures: recently, one site that cost £6 million to set up was sold for £30,000. Consequently, most companies are using Web sites as part of a mixed-media marketing plan for 'awareness raising'.

Brian Cooper, Marketing Manager of Trinity College, says that the Internet is useful as an introduction. However, doing business with the world, he finds that in most cultures 'the people you do business with are the people you trust', and this trust is only built up via frequent face-to-face meetings.

Some sites have had unexpected success, particularly those servicing the rural market when farmers were isolated on farms during the foot and mouth outbreak. The post could get through, and housewives shopped for essential dry goods on the Net.

Pet food Internet companies have had limited success. In theory, as heavy dog food, large dog beds, etc are delivered to your door, pet owners should be signing up in droves. However, firms that started out with great plans have fallen by the wayside, principally because they spent millions on marketing but ignored distribution – and people kept waiting for goods tell friends (the worst PR!).

One successful Web company, www.petplanet.co.uk, concentrated on distribution before thinking of expansion. Their site offers information, shopping services and other pet-related issues under one roof, and is aimed at the pet lover as well as the more serious breeder. The site offers services from picking a pet to suit browsers' lifestyle, to purchasing pet products and services, and tests knowledge with weekly quizzes. The site is fast, user-friendly and easy to navigate (Microsoft could learn a thing or two!). Information is never more than a few clicks away, and the site has a helpful registration tool that takes note of where you live and uses this information to get you results specific to your area (handy when you are looking for kennels or pet-friendly holiday accommodation, for example).

The site grew by offering delivery the next day or a two- to three-day delivery service, with free standard delivery on orders of £45 or more. Online ordering is quick and simple via a secure Verisign encrypted line and the information is held safe using the latest firewall technology – PetPlanet is an accepted member of the Which? Web Traders Association and adheres to their code of practice, a fact that should calm fears of credit card misuse.

With over 5,000 pet related products, petplanet.co.uk supplies hard-to-find pet items, offering everything from Burberry trouser suits for pooches to organic cat food for the most discerning felines. When Passports for Pets came in, PetPlanet discovered that MAFF (the Ministry in charge) hadn't addressed the issue of what paperwork was needed for pets to enter other countries, so embarked on a massive exercise to gather information from the 18 countries originally in the scheme – then found the government site copied their information!

The site uses modern technology to offer free interactive expert advice from a team of vets, and access to informative articles regarding care and development. There is a bulletin board-based chat group with some fascinating information and articles on pet-related subjects: from the hotel that welcomes guests with goldfish in their rooms, to the world's first police dog force (in Belgium). The Web site also works closely with a large number of animal welfare charities that cooperate with PetPlanet's online rehoming scheme for animals in rescue centres. If you want to see how a Web site can be interactive, useful and sell – type in www.petplanet.co.uk and see for yourself!

Finding a job

In this industry the average age of employees is 26. People tend to find jobs by word of mouth via friends. One person working for lastminute.com was asked how he found his job, and replied, 'My wife went on a course with the founder.'

Networking seems to be the way in to work with the Internet; there are agencies that claim to supply jobs, but are gone before you even have time to log on. Try going to company Web sites, click on 'recruitment' or 'career' buttons – and you could be in a job.

Designing Web sites is an expanding freelance job, but finding the companies that want this carried out is difficult. Membership of a business club or local Chamber of Commerce is one way to network and find customers.

Setting up a site

As author of this book, I wanted to set up my own site to sell the training books and distance learning tourism courses I had written. Most Internet service providers (ISPs) offer 'free Web space', and everyone tells you their kid wrote their site. Yes, if I were a teenager I could probably devote weeks to designing my own Web site – but after the first three-hour session I realised it would be more sensible to use those hours to earn money and pay someone to write it for me! But if you want to design your own site, go on a course; contact your local Job Centre to find courses in your area.

To set up my site, firms quoted from £2,000 to £3,000, but one in the area suggested I employ their newest recruit – she could learn while she was developing my site, and it would cost a fraction of the fee. So Judy was given the brief: the site had to be quick to navigate, easy for foreigners as well as English speakers to use, and – unlike other sites – I did not want it to offer an e-mail contact. If people wanted more information they had to phone me on a premium-rate line that paid me for my time. Every caller always needs tailor-made attention, and it was costing too much time to service several 20- to 30-minute calls a day. Teachers had been giving out my telephone number and telling their students to phone me if they didn't know answers. See www.tourismtraining.biz to see if Judy has developed a simple site that gives out basic information in an easy-to-navigate formula.

The next step is to pay for site hosting, to be placed high up on search engine sites.

Setting up your office

Most people want to start setting up their home office as quickly as possible. So, do you start looking at ads for IT equipment? Er – no. Homeworkers say find out about helplines before buying any PCs, faxes, printers, etc. Product prices are going down – and so, often, is quality. Manuals are no help at all. So, find out:

- ◆ Does the helpline talk your language?
- ◆ Is it available when you want it?
- ◆ Is it a long-distance or overseas number, or local?
- ◆ Whether the company patches you through to helplines in other countries. Microsoft tried this, but found British people couldn't understand US accents.

One reason I like IBM is that they have a freephone number: 0800 169 1485.

Computers

Most IT advertising is aimed at either the large company *or* the computer buff. So, if you are buying a PC, don't let salespeople stun you with patter. Make a list of what features YOU want – not what the company wants to sell you.

When buying, use a credit card. Then if the company goes bust you have a safety net – and check that the warranty is backed by insurance to pay for repairs if the company folds. If you think you want a laptop but can't afford the cost, try a reconditioned IBM machine – I've used one myself and it worked beautifully.

Security

Make sure all your equipment is insured in the home and if you take it away. Laptop theft is frequent; it can be opportunist, or you might be targeted if you work on commercially sensitive projects. It is up to you to make sure your work is protected; if not, you could find clients suing you. If hackers can get into the Pentagon's and Prince Philip's computers, what could they do to you?

As IBM supply governments and armed forces around the world, I asked them for Top Tips to ensure your business is secure. Some of their advice may be too sophisticated for a small home office, but read what they have to say and adapt their suggestions:

◆ Make sure your laptop is adequately insured in the event of loss. Insurance usually covers cost of equipment, but not the cost of the intellectual capital stored on it. Machines are easy to replace, but consider the implications of sensitive client/company information getting into the wrong hands.

If a stolen or lost laptop ends up in the hands of a hacker, your company's data, your customers' records and your confidential contracts could leak out. Protect data on the system by encrypting it and controlling access.

For extra security IBM teams up with third party security suppliers such as Targus PC Fingerprint Solution, which can be integrated with IBM's Embedded Security Subsystem. The fingerprint image is protected by the security chip within the laptop, making this more than just a 'software only' solution.

◆ Passwords are integral to ensuring that only authorised users access your network. Remember them: passwords account for over 50 per cent of help-desk calls!

Cybercrime can be averted with IBM's Client Security Software, including support for optional fingerprint readers and proximity badges to verify user identity.

Be aware of the risks of e-mailing! E-mails can be read over the Internet by anyone with readily available 'sniffer' technology. So IBM recommends ensuring that your e-mails are encrypted so that they can't be accessed by hackers. Equally, hard drive files are at risk of being read over cable modem or DSL connections and can be accessed if your machine is stolen.

◆ Over the past year there has been a huge surge in mobile working, making it easier for people to access their internal networks and e-mail. It is important to consider the security of your data as it passes over a public network like the Internet. Wireless networks add a new level of security risks as data can be stolen by someone who is simply nearby. IBM recommend implementing additional security mechanisms such as strong user and system authentication, end-to-end encryption, virtual private networks (VPNs) and firewalls for any access from public places or wireless LANs and to protect corporate data.

◆ Back your system up regularly. Regular backups mean that data are protected from viruses, theft or even hardware malfunctions. If something goes wrong, IBM's Rapid Restore system can restore a system in 15–20 minutes. Rapid Restore can be downloaded for free from IBM's support Web site.

Invest in anti-virus software. My IBM ThinkPad came preloaded with Norton Anti-Virus, and I also invested in Norton CleanSweep.

Cameras

If you use a camera for work, you will probably need to insure it separately; it may not be covered by household insurance. If you want to shoot slides for a presentation, today's little AutoZoom cameras do a big job.

E-mail and fax machines

Putting your e-mail address on your cards or letterhead can be asking for trouble – you are at the mercy of companies sending junk mail. If you need to use a fax, Brother make simple machines and their helpline is helpful.

Money

If you are aged 18–30 and have been refused money by a bank to set up your business, try The Prince's Trust (0800 842 842). Another possibility is Small Firms Training Loans (0800 132 6600; www.lifelonglearning.dfes.gov.uk).

Phones

Phones will probably be your most important business tool. You must have a reliable message service, and it is worthwhile looking at BT's Ultimate 106 home telephone system if you are going to share incoming lines with the rest of the family. It separates your messages and you can check these when away from home.

You will probably sign up to one of the 170-plus telephone companies offering cheap calls, as currently BT daytime calls are more expensive, but ask friends which companies they use. I am not going to recommend a company – just say I used to recommend Mercury, which changed to ntl. Their wonderful service changed too, and I ended up pulling the plug when they cut me off for the third time for non-payment even though they had cashed my cheques!

Cordless phones

Calls from cordless phones cost the same as on an ordinary line, but you can carry the phone around at home. 'Bolt on' a BT Diverse Repeater and you have a range of around 500 metres if you want to go down to the bottom of the garden. Incidentally, the 'Diverse' range are all digital, meaning that they give clear reception.

Mobile phones

Do you really need a mobile phone? You don't see top people carrying them, and mobile phone theft is becoming a prevalent crime. But if you do need one, look carefully at costs and after-sales service. Adverts trumpet 'calls cost 1p per minute', but small print says this is only after 6pm – not much use for business calls. If you have a mobile, make sure it can be used in whichever country you work. Ian Volens from OnetoOne says that the minimum you need is dual-band capability for Europe and tri-band capability for the United States.

Top Tips

If you need to make reversed charge calls, ntl DO NOT offer this facility.

Wires

If you use a desktop PC, invest in a Logitech keyboard and mouse. Radio technology means there are no trailing wires to clutter up your desk.

Useful telephone numbers

I am not recommending these companies, just mentioning them because in the past they have been helpful to the SOHO market. Do remember to get different quotations, and don't just look at the price – check what end benefits you receive.

- ◆ BT 0800 800 150;
- ◆ Brother 0845 6060 626;
- ◆ Olympus 020 7253 2772;
- ◆ Symantec (for Norton AntiVirus) 020 7616 5600;
- ◆ Viking (for home stationery deliveries) 0800 424444;
- ◆ Wick Hill (firewalls) 01483 466500.

8 Courses and qualifications

Although success in marketing, advertising and PR depends much more on personal qualities than on qualifications, you need to get a job in the first place. Most recruiters look for graduates, or equivalent, with first-class degrees or doctorates. If no one suitable comes forth, they will then look for an HND in design, sandwich degree in business, etc. So you need to look carefully at the opportunities and options available for continuing your education after leaving school. However, everyone agrees that it is you as a person, plus your experience, that counts. It is possible to work your way up from the lowliest researcher, and if you are a woman returner or starting a second career, there are jobs available – but you have to fight for these when the 'raw' person recruiters look for first is educated to graduate level.

Help and advice about qualifications and courses are available from your school, college or local authority careers service. It is important that you speak to people who understand the commercial world and the local and national education and employment scene. If you know people who work in marketing or related areas, speak to them too.

Before you attend an interview or advice session with a careers adviser, think about yourself, your ambitions and how you plan to realise them. The more they know about you and the further down the road you are, the more time you will save and the more useful your session. Write down your ideas and some form of CV, however basic, before you go.

Once you have your degree and are working in the appropriate area you may want to continue with professional qualifications awarded by the institutes that govern marketing, advertising and PR.

If you do not have a degree-level qualification, there are other routes into the business, although not such clear career paths. It is possible to transfer across to one of these areas of work once you are already in another type of job, often by taking professional qualifications in your spare time.

This chapter looks at the qualifications you are likely to need to get a job in these areas, alternative 'back door' routes, plus the professional training to consider once you are in. For more information about courses, contact trainers and colleges.

Age 16–18

You may be taking purely academic subjects at GCSE (SCE Standard Grade in Scotland) and going on to appropriate A/AS levels. These are often the qualifications understood by interviewers.

Or you could be taking a vocational qualification such as a GNVQ (General National Vocational Qualification). GNVQs are popular with colleges but had a poor reception from employers. Recently, they have been revised to be more in line with what employers require.

GNVQs are offered by the main assessment bodies (OCR, AQA, and EdExcel). They are not all the same; some units have been written by those in the industry, so are more appropriate if you want an idea of what the work involves. Probably the most suitable GNVQs are in Art and Design, Business, Tourism, IT, Media, Retail and Distributive Services.

If you want to work in the conference and event sector, investigate the new Vocational Qualification for Conference and Event Staff. This is a practical course offered in colleges around Britain, devised by those working in the industry – so they know what is required. Sadly, many GNVQs are project based, meaning that college tutors tell you, say, to 'draw up a plan for a 2,000-delegate international conference'. As the tutor has never worked in this sector, no one knows if your plan is going to work – but you probably get a mark based on the thickness of the paperwork you have submitted. Cynical, but employers in the industry don't rate these qualifications. How often do you see a job advert asking for GNVQs?

Top Tips

If you want some practical experience to put on your CV, contact a major charity such as the RNLI, Red Cross, RNIB or Royal National Institute for Deaf People. They all have information packs and back-up support to help you organise an event.

Sue Ockwell, PR for AITO (the Association of Independent Tour Operators), says charity work is highly regarded on CVs. Read the *Intermediate GNVQ Textbook for Leisure and Tourism* (Addison Wesley Longman, ISBN 0 582 27841 4), which has a case study on running a flag day and the basic knowledge you need to run incentive and other conferences.

For NVQs for the events industry, contact ESITO. NVQs (National Vocational Qualifications; SVQs in Scotland) are work-based competencies measuring knowledge and under-standing that individuals hold in their heads, skills they possess and whether they can apply this knowledge and understanding to carry out a job. You can learn how to do a job in college or university, but a vocational qualification tests if you can actually carry out this job to an employer's satisfaction.

To take an NVQ you don't have to be working; you can take courses at a college, but these must include work placement with an appropriate employer. Role-playing or working in a college office doesn't count. Before you sign up for a course, find out what links colleges have with industry and where you will be doing your work placement.

18-plus

At this stage, you can take a first degree, a diploma of higher education (DipHE), Higher National Diploma or Certificate (HND or HNC).

Recruiters in marketing, advertising and public relations are, as this book continually points out, looking for your personality rather than your degree area. Studying for a marketing-related degree indicates that you plan to enter marketing as a career; assuming you obtain a decent degree, this will help.

However, if you have the attributes employers are looking for, recruiters for many of the jobs covered by this book won't care whether your degree was in history or biochemistry.

Remember, though, that there are some jobs that require background study. In market research you need to show an ability with figures and demonstrate your ease with systems work. For the creative side of advertising you may need an art or design degree. Yet even here, once you are in work, you may find yourself swapping roles within the creative team, with the words person having significant input on the visual side.

The London Chamber of Commerce and Industry (LCCI) runs Third Level Diploma courses in Advertising, Public Relations, Marketing and Purchasing. These diplomas meet the entry requirements for the CAM Certificate and most higher education institutions recognise LCCI qualifications.

After a degree or equivalent qualification

If you are already in higher education you might be interested in courses run by the Chartered Institute of Marketing (CIM) and the Communication, Advertising and Marketing Education Foundation (CAM), which represents the 11 trade and professional associations in advertising, public relations and allied businesses listed on page 75.

You do not need to work in a related area to study for further qualifications, although this is usual. Less than 4 per cent of CAM students are working for their qualifications full time, for example. Others may be planning a career change and taking the courses as a means into a new job.

Some of the qualifications on offer qualify you for membership of the appropriate professional body. Membership is also dependent on working a certain time in the appropriate commercial area. Check with the relevant professional body whether your chosen qualification would be appropriate for membership. Other qualifications may help you to work towards membership or may simply help train you to do your job better. See below for more details of professional courses and qualifications.

Other ways in

You might consider yourself to be every marketing or PR manager's idea of a perfect recruit yet not hold good enough or appropriate academic qualifications. What then? In work areas that stress your personal qualities, surely there must be ways in for the academically less qualified? There are certainly many support roles in any marketing, advertising or PR department or agency. Starting in the mail room may not sound glamorous, but if you are sure you want a career in these areas and cannot get the appropriate qualifications, it could be worth a try. The same goes for secretarial support or any other role that puts you in contact with the core workers in the organisation. Remember that you could be in for a long haul and that there are no guarantees – but then there are none even if you join the elite graduate intake; if you don't perform, you're out.

Top Tips

Join a temporary secretarial agency close to ad agencies. Once you have a foot in an agency's door you are on the spot to hear about jobs.

Government schemes

There are several government-funded training schemes for school leavers, giving the opportunity to train as you gain experience. It is worthwhile contacting the Learning and Skills Council or Small Business Service for details.

Although there is no specific training currently available in marketing, advertising and PR, signing on for Youth Training or a Modern Apprenticeship in Information Technology or Business Administration could take you into the heart of a working marketing, advertising or PR business. You need to select your employer carefully to ensure the job is as near as possible to the type of work you want to do.

In the eyes of many employers, New Deal, the government's £3 billion scheme to help the unemployed into a job, has been a failure. Twice press officers at the Department of Work and Pensions referred me to another department, saying it wasn't their scheme. Well, it is, and theoretically they have various schemes to help people into work: youngsters, lone parents, disabled, 50-plus, etc. Press reports point to a poor job retention rate, but if you qualify, and are very persistent, you might find this scheme helpful – but then if you are that persistent, you would probably find a job anyway.

Courses and entrance requirements

Once you have gained A levels or equivalent qualifications, ask relevant industry associations about the courses available.

Remember that once you are out of full-time education LEA funding is not automatic, so either you or your employer must pay for your tuition.

Business-related full-time courses

A business qualification is helpful in getting a job and understanding the work more easily once in. That does not mean you necessarily need a business studies degree or similar. Plenty of people go into marketing with degrees, HNDs, etc in other subjects. It does, however, show that you are committed and have a theoretical understanding of business concepts.

Recruiters are increasingly interested in your relevant work experience and see the 'filling' of a sandwich course as excellent grounding. This is as good a reason for choosing a vocational course as the actual lecture content. Yet the qualification in itself is not everything – if it means dropping a favourite subject, ask yourself if it is worth it. It is a *combination* of your experience, attitude, personality and degree class that gets you the job; only a part of that is your degree subject.

Market research jobs usually require a high level of numeracy; a number-based degree demonstrates this. Employers generally look for good computer skills and an analytical approach rather than applied maths or numerical analysis degrees, so a well-chosen business-related course will serve just as well, remembering that it is those personal qualities and experience that will land you the job.

People looking at the creative side of marketing and advertising should read the later section on art and design courses.

Degrees

If you want to study for a degree with a marketing, PR or advertising content, you are more likely to find what you want at a new university, as these tend to offer courses allied to vocational needs. Old universities are heading this way, though, so look around.

Many courses are made up of a range of options related to a central theme. Some are sandwich courses, where you spend at least one year of a four-year course in employment related to your field of study; these are popular with future employers.

It has become more difficult in recent years to ensure that all sandwich students are allotted places in companies and other organisations, and some students have found themselves in jobs which are not closely related to what they hope to do. Nevertheless, any period of work experience is useful and you can find out about an organisation's marketing structure even if working in another capacity. It might be worth asking for a list of previous sandwich placements when going for interview and assessing which will be best for you.

Some courses are modular, where you design your own course from a broad choice of options. In Scotland a broader-based, four-year degree course is the norm.

Other business courses

You can keep your options open by choosing the broader two-year Diploma of Higher Education, and possibly work for an additional one or two years afterwards to make it up to a degree.

Look through the index of the UCAS Handbook for some idea of the breadth of choice in business-related courses. Send for prospectuses and consult a guide such as the *Compendium of Higher Education* (Trotman) for more information.

Business-related part-time courses

You may be able to study for your degree or HND on a part-time basis. Once you have graduated and are in work you can continue studying, perhaps to gain specific expertise or to apply for membership of one of the professional bodies.

Professional qualifications

The Chartered Institute of Marketing (CIM) is 'an internation-ally recognised catalyst for the improvement of marketing skills to the benefit of members, their companies and others in the marketing profession', with three levels of qualification: Certificate, Advanced Certificate and Diploma, the latter quali-fying students for membership.

You can obtain the Diploma by one of two routes. The marketing route involves completion of the Certificate in Marketing, the Advanced Certificate in Marketing and then the

Diploma in Marketing. The sales route involves the Certificate in Selling, the Advanced Certificate in Sales Management and finally the Diploma in Marketing. Each level is designed to be achievable with one year of part-time study. There are exemptions at all levels and if you have a relevant business degree with the appropriate marketing options you may not have to sit any exams at all for membership. You also need relevant work experience.

Courses are run by the Institute itself and also by organisations such as the National Extension College, which allows you to study at your own pace with distance learning.

As well as courses run to help students become members, there are many technical and development courses run by the Institute, covering every aspect of marketing theory and practice. If you are interested in working in tourism, many tour operators see a marketing qualification as more useful than 'tourism' courses.

Communication, Advertising and Marketing Education Foundation (CAM)

CAM was set up to administer exams for a number of professional bodies working in the same broad field. These are:

- Advertising Association;
- Advertising Standards Authority;
- Association of Independent Radio Companies;
- Cinema Advertising Association;
- Direct Marketing Association;
- Exhibition Liaison Committee;
- Incorporated Society of British Advertisers;
- Institute of Public Relations;
- Institute of Sales Promotion;
- ITV Network Centre;
- Public Relations Consultants Association.

There is a Certificate, taken by students of any of these disciplines, and a Diploma, which is discipline specific. Again, there are exemptions based on previous study. As an example, the

Institute of Public Relations publishes a list of educational qualifications approved for membership such as the CAM Diploma in Public Relations, and offered at recommended colleges in Britain. CAM courses can be taken part time or by distance learning from a large number of colleges.

National Film and Television School

One of the world's leading centres for professional training in the screen entertainment and media industries, the NFTS runs full-time MA courses in animation, fiction or documentary direction, screenwriting, producing, screen design, cinematography, editing, sound, post-production and screen music. Courses are strongly production oriented and replicate industry working practices. Many new graduates work on commercials and pop promos as well as TV productions and feature films.

Membership of professional bodies

Any meeting of professionals gives you a chance to network – an effective way to find out about different jobs and what is available. Contacts might offer you work experience or even a job – it happens. Become a student member of relevant associations and take advantage of meetings, AGMs, etc.

For full membership of professional associations, the courses and qualifications described above are relevant for most marketing and related careers. As well as gaining qualifications or being exempt from them, you need to demonstrate a period of time spent working in the relevant area. To join the CIM, for instance, you need a minimum of three years' experience.

Members of the IPA represent 80 per cent of UK billings. To become a personal member you need to have at least five years' experience with a member agency. You do not need any specific qualifications.

The Advertising Association does not have individual members but is an umbrella association for 27 trade members within advertising.

The Institute of Direct Marketing represents a more specialist area of the profession.

When choosing subjects to study, remember that many people change their career aims over the years; if you give up subjects you love for those you feel are necessary, you could regret not having continued if you change your mind later. If in doubt, keep your choices broad and discuss this with your careers adviser.

Entrance requirements for professional qualifications

For courses leading to membership of one of the marketing-related professional bodies, contact the appropriate institute or association. Generally, the exams set by the professional bodies start at a fairly basic level, so if you leave school with good GCSE/SCE grades you should find a suitable study route. The IPA does not require any qualifications for membership, just relevant experience. If you are at sixth form level you should check whether your proposed higher education course will give you exemption from professional courses or exams.

Design-related courses

Entrance to almost all higher education art and design courses above foundation level in England, Wales and Northern Ireland is administered by Art and Design Route A and B (part of UCAS). Some Scottish institutions also use ADAR.

As well as fine art, courses including computer graphics, video production, etc are useful for people looking at the creative side of advertising. Some courses are modular, allowing you to choose non-art or design subjects as part of one qualification. You could choose business studies in your HND in advertising (copywriting and art direction).

UCAS processes applications for different types of qualification and degrees, HNDs and a few DipHEs. For foundation-level courses, apply direct to the college concerned and remember that your LEA may only fund your foundation course if it is taken at one of its colleges.

Who needs an art or design qualification?

Working as a 'creative' (eg a designer or art director) you need a certain eye and creative ability. Your first job in an agency may involve visualising advertising ideas, so some hands-on skills are important. As you progress, you are less likely to be involved at this level but still need a creative mind and an ability to express this.

Copywriters, too, need that creative flair, but it is equally possible to enter advertising as a copywriter with a degree or equivalent in any other subject (or indeed after a spell in the print room, although, as discussed earlier, this approach is less likely to succeed than coming through the mainstream routes).

Designers are needed to produce product packaging; an important commercial area and constantly needing new blood. *Design Courses* (Trotman) lists different types of course by general subject area.

Many higher education, design-related courses can be taken part time. Look at *Design Courses*. Once you are in a job your employer may want to train you on in certain aspects of your work. Contact the Designers and Art Directors Association to find out more about professional training.

Entrance requirements for design-related courses

Many art and design-related degree and HND course tutors select students from one-year art and design foundation courses run by colleges around the country. You need this year to bring on your technical skills and give you time to produce a portfolio for degree course selection.

A look through the UCAS *Handbook* will show you that most course tutors do not select straight from school. There are some courses designed primarily for mature applicants and tutors may consider mature applicants with different qualifications for other courses.

Distance learning and short courses in all subjects

Designed to let you study at home in your own time and at your own pace, distance learning courses are useful for people going into marketing-related careers. Sometimes it is possible to 'mix and match' by taking a course with a summer school, a seminar or perhaps a tutorial system with local help.

If you take a correspondence course, make sure the college is endorsed by the Council for the Accreditation of Correspondence Colleges or a similar organisation. A list of accredited colleges can be found in the *Education Yearbook* in your local reference library, or contact Learning Direct for details.

Top Tips

Media studies courses are popular with students and colleges, but not with employers. They see these as catch-all courses leading to unemployment in a vastly overpopulated sector. If you take this course, ask searching questions about job experience as part of the course.

Short courses

CIM, CAM, the Institute of Direct Marketing and the Direct Marketing Association run courses on all aspects of marketing for those working in the industry, leading to membership exams.

As well as the UCAS *Handbook*, look in the trade publications for colleges running short, full- or part-time courses for any of these CAM, CIM and LCCI courses. These organisations will also supply you with details of colleges running their courses.

Short courses in related areas

The Publishing Training Centre at Book House (the industry training organisation for the publishing industry) runs training for people working in the publishing industry and offers copy-writing workshops.

Languages

Knowledge of a business language is becoming more and more important. One of the best ways of learning a language is working overseas. If you are looking for work during a gap year it is probably sensible to look in a country with a 'useful' language. CILT (the Centre for Information on Language Teaching and Research) and the National Business Language Information Service can give more details on courses and qualifications.

You may be reluctant to learn another language because you are embarrassed about speaking in front of others. European students learn pronunciation as a matter of course; many of their schools use the Auralog system. You can use this too – you just need a PC with loudspeakers. Sit in front of the screen and answer questions verbally from a speech recognition program. A graph shows you where you are going wrong, helps you get the pronunciation right and then sends you to the next stage – a fun way of learning a language whilst sparing your blushes.

In this industry English speakers have an advantage: it is the international language of contact and non-native English speakers often have to prove that they speak business English. If English isn't your mother tongue, Trinity College offers graded assessments in communication, which can be more useful than paper-based exams. For example, if you want to work in marketing in the conference, PR and events sector, you can take a Certificate in Effective Communication for Events.

Which course?

The best way to decide on a suitable course is to ask those in the industry which they recommend. If they can't help, contact UCAS or look on the ECCTIS computer database. Your school or college careers library, local reference library and local authority careers office should have copies of the reference books you need and may also have college prospectuses.

Remember to look into the financial situation early if you are applying for a grant, especially if you are hoping for extra finance from sponsorship for study abroad, etc.

Look at taking a course in another area, perhaps not leading directly into marketing, advertising or PR but leading to a parallel course. You might work in publishing, for instance, then move across to advertising at a later stage, or freelance as an assistant for a photographer or film producer, or do temporary work with agencies in marketing.

Courses are also run at colleges and centres as part of the adult education programme, especially for those setting up their own business. 'Starting a small business' or 'business start-up' courses are often run on a one evening per week basis. These do not lead directly to any qualification but could be a useful extra to give you some idea of how a small business works and the role of marketing within it. Contact Business Link or the Learning and Skills Council for details.

For postgraduate study details, contact the appropriate professional body.

There are specialised training courses such as the copywriting workshop run by the Publishing Training Centre – a two-day course on copywriting. Tuition on these courses is intense, with small classes. Fees around £250 per day reflect that normally these courses are taken by people already working – with their firms picking up the bill. However, this might be a good way of networking your way into the industry. Associations and trade press will have details of other courses.

Preparation

Work experience is vital on your CV. It shows that you are:

- seriously committed;
- able to organise and motivate yourself;
- aware of what work is about;
- able to hold down a job/placement;
- therefore employable.

Whilst you are still at school or in further education, think about your own experience and how you can improve on it.

Some employers are set up to offer work experience but many do not have the resources. You are not going to be useful to an employer if you are only there for a week or two. If you are looking for a career in mainstream marketing, getting a placement may be relatively easy, as the marketing departments of large organisations are more likely to have the resources (staff, time, enough simple jobs) to cope.

Small companies, including many advertising, sales promotion and market research agencies, have few staff – so their time is precious. If there is no training manager, just the procedure of finding the right person to supervise you can be a headache.

This doesn't mean you should give up – on the contrary, the harder it is, the harder you need to try. The more initiative you show, the better candidate you will be when applying for courses and jobs. Start now, by contacting the person who arranges work experience placements, and keep asking until you are sure that the first suitable one to come up goes to you (using your very best communication skills, of course – if you simply annoy them you'll be at the bottom of their list, not the top).

Look in your local library for a copy of *Hollis UK Press and Public Relations Annual* or the *Advertisers Annual*. Both contain thousands of contacts – it is a question of sifting through and using some creative thought to approach them and say why YOU would be an asset to their company.

Remember: to be employable, you must have keyboard skills and know how to operate modern office equipment.

If you have already carried out a placement, look around for another – the more experience you get, the better. Try a few different types of work and some different types of employer. Remember, of course, to keep a work diary and write up notes at the end of each placement on:

◆ the work;
◆ the sector (public, private, large/small organisation, etc);
◆ the management;
◆ yourself;
◆ your career aspirations.

Preparing for a business-related course

As well as the necessary academic ability and experience, you need to demonstrate the right personal qualities to persuade an admissions tutor to give you a reasonable course offer. The more the tutor wants you, the better the offer you will receive. It is worth planning ahead and thinking exactly what they look for.

If aiming for a general course – a business studies degree, say – then you need to have thought out why you are applying for this particular course and get some relevant experience. Helping in any small business such as a shop is useful.

If you want to do a more specific course, such as one devoted to advertising or marketing, or with an option, you need to show that you are interested and active in these fields. You can't expect to get a place on a highly competitive course without showing some experience – selling ads in the holidays, perhaps, or setting up or publishing the school mag. As well as the experience itself you need to explain why you did it, what it has given you and why you should be chosen.

Look again at your personal qualities. Brush up those aspects of your personal skills that do not quite meet the mark and do a little personal development. Helping out with a charity is often helpful; employers like this experience on a CV. It's not just employers who want to see your personal qualities shine through – admissions tutors do too.

Preparing for an art or design course

Before applying for an art or design course, look carefully at
your abilities, experience and determination. Most people start
with a year's art foundation course to prepare them for entry to
a degree course. Although this is not essential, selection for
degree-level courses is not based simply on your A level art
grade, but on the work that you present for assessment, as well
as your personality. If it is still a year or two before you are going
to start making applications, then it is worth thinking very hard
about this route – although entry to foundation courses is not
too competitive, competition at the next stage, to the art degree
or equivalent proper, is intense.

Preparation checklist

- ◆ Arrange a careers counselling session.
- ◆ Follow this up with more research into your chosen area:
  ring or write to the appropriate professional bodies. (If
  they charge for information packs, perhaps you could see
  if your careers office will buy them.)
- ◆ Talk to everyone you know in a 'communications' job.
- ◆ Arrange work experience through tutors or arrange this
  yourself in conjunction with your school/college contact.
- ◆ Set up your own communications business – starting a
  school newsletter, for instance – or any enterprise
  involving sales – car washing, gardening, selling craft items
  and so on. Make sure you have appropriate supervision
  and always tell someone responsible what you are doing
  and where you will be.
- ◆ Telephone or write to employers in your chosen field,
  asking for recruitment literature and other details of their
  recruitment and training. Remember to send a stamped
  addressed envelope as many small companies can't afford a
  large postage bill. Ask whether any of them will see you
  for an informal chat for careers counselling or mentoring
  – think of good reasons why they would want to do this.
- ◆ Get along to any relevant events – recruitment fairs,
  marketing launches, exhibitions, etc, even those aimed at a

different audience. Get what you can from them in the way of experience and tips for your career and job search.

♦ See if there is a broadcasting course run on a subsidised basis by local colleges or your local radio station.

♦ If you are interested in photography, see if there are competitions you can enter in your local paper or magazines. Membership of the Bureau of Freelance Photographers (approx. £40 p.a.) can be useful. Their monthly newsletter often has competition details.

Choosing your course

1. Are your academic qualifications good enough for the course you are considering?
2. Vocational or general course? Look back over your experience, see what you enjoyed most and talk to parents and tutors.
3. Give sandwich placements serious thought.
4. If you think you are not academic enough for a degree or equivalent, look carefully at the other courses available and the training options once in work.
5. Do you want to spend some time abroad? Contact ERASMUS (before you apply for courses) for information about their programmes within the European Union.
6. If you are in work, check out the possibilities for part-time and day-release study. The amount of support you get often makes all the difference – work on your employer for help with fees, study time, and block and day release.
7. Check whether your preferred qualification is suitable for your career and whether it gives you exemption from professional exams. Look at *British Qualifications* (Kogan Page), and speak to course tutors and the relevant professional body.

Researching for the right course

Read *Which Degree?* (Hobsons), the *Compendium of Advanced Courses in Colleges of Further and Higher Education* and the *Directory of UK Higher Education*, all available at the reference library, plus any other books they have that may be useful. You can also access ECCTIS, a computerised information service covering over 100,000 course opportunities in all colleges of further and higher education, through your careers office.

Send for prospectuses from colleges and universities which interest you, enclosing a gummed stamped addressed label if possible – not an envelope. Visit your top choices (phone before you arrive to make an appointment). A Young Person's Coachcard gives you up to 30 per cent discount on fares across Britain. Remember, the course content is more important than the place. Talk to current students taking the course.

Disabled students

Institutions of higher education are sympathetic to the requirements of applicants with disabilities and other needs and are anxious to provide appropriate support. Many have developed equal opportunities policies and practices.

Before making a formal application, contact the institution direct to discuss any support needs you may have. Explain the nature and extent of your disability and mention any particular arrangements you have found helpful in the past. It is a good idea to arrange an informal visit to assess the difficulties of access and to discuss your needs with the staff. Your application will be considered on the same criteria as any other candidate and any medical information will be kept confidential.

Contact the Information Service of Skill: National Bureau for Students with Disabilities for personal advice and up-to-date information on all aspects of applying for a course. It publishes a series of leaflets giving helpful information about various aspects of studying with a disability. The Bureau can also give information about the colleges which have special facilities and purpose-built accommodation.

Financing your studies

Your careers adviser will be able to give you more information, particularly if there are any local grants available. It is worth while looking at some of the following schemes – but sometimes the paperwork takes so long, you would be better off taking a Saturday job to earn the money instead.

Career development loans for those aged 18 and over are administered by the Department for Education and Skills in partnership with banks (0800 585505).

Employers and professional bodies offer sponsorship schemes – consult Student Sponsorship Information Service's free leaflet *A Question of Sponsorship?* and the *Which? Guide to Sponsorship in Higher Education*.

For details of educational trust funds and charities, refer to the *Charities Digest*, published by Waterlows (020 7342 2354) at £23.95, or *Education Grants Directory*, published by Directory of Social Change (020 7209 5151) at £19.95.

For details of European Union programmes such as SOCRATES-ERASMUS, incorporating LINGUA for foreign language study, contact UK ERASMUS Student Grants Council (020 7489 1992).

Access funds and hardship grants are administered by individual colleges.

Full details about grants and loans are given in the DfES leaflet *Student Grants and Loans: A brief guide*, available free from DfES Publications Centre (0800 731 7133), and, for Scottish students, *Student Grants in Scotland: A guide to undergraduate allowances* from the Scottish Education Department. In Northern Ireland, a *Guide to Awards and Loans to Students* is available from the Department of Education. Your LEA may publish its own version of these guides.

The Educational Grants Advisory Service, part of the Family Welfare Association, has an educational grants adviser who gives telephone advice.

What's it like?

We all need advertising, marketing and PR – although we may not realise it. Sometimes people working in these sectors might question this themselves. If you come back from a pitch feeling you weren't able to get over your ideas to the client, and several weeks' unpaid work (for your company) have probably been for nothing, remember the old adage that this work is 5 per cent inspiration and 95 per cent perspiration.

Top Tips

Charity shops sometimes need window dressers to make their windows look more enticing – good practice!

How to get a job

Wendy Carter, who recruits for the giant J. Walter Thompson agency, says it depends on the current vacancies what degrees, skills or relevant qualifications applicants need. Trainees start in service departments such as finance or the knowledge centre (library information centre). 'It is a competitive industry and if you aren't a graduate you have to be good – exceptionally good.' When recruiting, she looks for a 'feel' for the industry and advises applying to as many agencies as possible.

At the risk of sounding repetitive: it's not easy to get a job in this sector; you have to be very, very determined. The Institute of Practitioners in Advertising (IPA) says applications from graduates exceed vacancies by a ratio of around 10:1. Fewer than 50 agencies recruit graduates regularly; these are listed in the IPA *Factfile* (send a large sae to the IPA – address in Chapter 10 – for a copy).

What captures recruiters' attention?

- ◆ A 'feel' for the industry can be developed and honed by studying advertising.
- ◆ Ask friends which ads interest them.
- ◆ Which ads interest your parents' generation?
- ◆ Listen to people talking in the bus or a queue.
- ◆ What makes you buy a product?
- ◆ Listen and learn.

New business studies courses are being developed in higher education each year. Many include a strong marketing element, with the possibility of specialising in advertising, marketing, design or PR. Even though there are more of these courses than ever before, there are more candidates with similar academic qualifications, so employers look for work experience as well as paper qualifications and enthusiasm.

At a time when many organisations have cut down on the number of new recruits, you may find it easier to get work experience if you offer to work for nothing. As well as contacting companies, approach charities. They don't welcome 'do-gooders'; but if you offer to do some focused market research, design inexpensive posters, analyse their direct mailing operation, look at their shop windows or revamp displays, you could find yourself with an interesting and worthwhile project that stands out on your CV. Typing and word-processing skills are the norm nowadays and any work should hone these to an acceptable standard.

Job advertisements

National papers feature media and marketing recruitment pages, especially the *Guardian* on Mondays. Specialist press, such as *Campaign*, *Marketing Week*, *Media Week*, *PR Week*, the *UK Press Gazette* and *Marketing*, carry recruitment advertising, usually for more senior positions, which offers an excellent insight into movements in the industry, who is working on which accounts, which agencies are successful, who is moving where and so on.

There are industry handbooks, yearbooks and directories with details of companies you could send speculative letters and CVs. These include:

- *The Advertisers Annual* (Hollis);
- *BRAD Advertiser and Agency List* (EMAP);
- *The Creative Handbook* (Variety Media Publications);
- *Hollis UK Press and Public Relations Annual*;
- *The Institute of Public Relations Handbook* (Kogan Page);

- *The Marketing Manager's Handbook* (AP Information Services);
- *Yellow Pages* and similar local publications.

Speculative applications

When you approach companies, phone the human resources department (modern-speak for personnel) to ask how they like applications. Do they:

- send out an e-mail application form;
- ask you to send an sae; or
- ask for CV and covering letter?

Do whatever they ask – companies like information presented their way and often don't have time to trawl through CVs.

Traineeships

If companies operate trainee schemes, places are often oversubscribed and preference is shown to graduates. The relevant association may have up-to-the-minute details of types of vacancies in their sector. *GO Directory*, published by Newpoint, lists employers offering training schemes to graduates in all areas of industry. See what careers advice and vacancy information publications are available from your local college or careers service, who may also be able to help you apply. Don't just consider working in major cities: a local company or agency may be able to offer a place.

Professional bodies

Professional bodies exist to help their members, and helping good people to enter the profession does just that. IPR produces sheets of information and advice on experience and job searching, and has a free counselling service using local practitioners. The Institute of Practitioners in Advertising publishes the *IPA Factfile* on its Web site (www.ipa.co.uk), listing the 50 or so agencies that run structured training schemes. When you log on, type 'guest' in the registration procedure.

Top Tips

There are many small local agencies that may not be members of the IPA. Try the *Yellow Pages*.

Telephone or write to the appropriate professional body for any information it may be able to send you. CIM has a very good handbook – send an sae.

Moving on or across

One ever-popular area is advertising sales. This involves a great deal of telephone work, trying to persuade people to advertise in a particular publication. It can be tough work, often for a low basic salary augmented by possible commission on sales. (Be careful about jobs offering commission only; it might be weeks before you make a sale and earn some money.) Nevertheless, it can get you into the media environment, particularly if you are working in a large organisation. Employers will also train you in skills you'll find invaluable later on. You can show your willingness to learn about marketing from the other side. Use this work to learn about advertising and audience research from the clients you book and the data you use to convince them to place their ads with your company.

Top Tips

Working in a newspaper or magazine's classified jobs section means you are the first to hear of vacancies.

Making your application

Make sure your CV and covering letter are error-free and that they read well. Good writing skills, attention to detail and presentation are important. Ensure that you have made the most of your work experience and relate it to the job you apply for. If you have already done some copywriting or press work, send in selected samples. Above all, try to get the balance right between essential information and too much detail. If you can, ask somebody working in a similar field to look at your CV and letter to give you an insider's view.

Above all, find out about the organisation before you write, and especially if you are invited for interview. They are likely to ask you what you thought of some of their recent work and to comment on work you have admired produced by other organisations or agencies. You must be aware of the industry's activity and be prepared to comment on it.

If you are going for a design position, you will need a smart portfolio with a limited number of strong pieces, presented in a way that shows you know what that company is looking for.

Read *Preparing Your Own CV*, by Rebecca Corfield (Kogan Page).

Top Tips

Every time you buy a product, analyse what made you buy.

Interviews

There are many books to give you advice about what to do in an interview. Once you have read them, remember that the impact you make as you walk into the room is extremely important. Then take note what Caroline Swain, Director of Professional Services at Right Management Consultants, says:

Attend the interview with a different focus. Ask yourself, is this the right job for me, at the right company, with the right future? By changing your approach, you will conquer your nerves and begin to assess the opportunity as much as the interviewer is assessing you. In this frame of mind you will be asking intelligent, searching questions and demonstrating your abilities in the process.

It ain't what you say, it's the way that you say it. It's said 75 per cent of communication is non-verbal. Being aware of your body language will help you come across well to the interviewer. Make eye contact. Smile. Give a firm handshake and mirror the interviewer's posture.

You want to look your best, especially as you will feel everyone in the agency is cool, hip, smart, chic – everything you want to be. So how do you get the look? Can you afford it? Yes, if you follow sassy media people to 'nearly new' shops such as Oxfam or London's Cheval Place, where shops offer 'nearly new' designer clothes at low prices.

Salaries and prospects

Salaries depend on the size of the organisation, its location and the generosity of the management. They also depend on the labour market and, fortunately, after weathering the recession, there seems to be a strong demand for good people.

Salary bands are near impossible to quote correctly. Your best indication is to look at the advertisements in the trade press. Job titles in these advertisements can be confusing – try to see how many years' experience the recruiters are looking for as an indication of the seniority of the post.

In very general terms, a marketing or public relations assistant in a first job after leaving college could expect a salary of £12,000 upwards. An executive with two years' experience could be looking at £16,000–£20,000 plus and a manager £22,000–£40,000. In advertising or sales promotion agencies a new account handler might earn between £13,000 and £18,000 and a copywriter or designer roughly the same.

Although the number of high earners has taken a nosedive since the mad 1980s, top people are still highly sought after and salaries reflect this. Salaries at this level are not normally disclosed in the recruitment advertisements – in fact, ads are often unnecessary, especially in the agencies, where word of mouth and previous campaigns can be the only CV you need. Senior staff may also be headhunted.

Below is a sample of recent job advertisements that highlight some of the skills sought and the salaries commanded by people at various stages of their career. Some unfamiliar terms are explained in the Glossary.

Marketing

Marketing Assistant. £12,000–£14,000 plus bonus. Lateral thinking, creative flair, business acumen and unlimited drive. You've got them all, plus a real passion for fashion. What you don't have is much practical experience to back your marketing degree.

Marketing Manager. c.£40,000 plus car plus benefits. An energetic, talented, multiple retail marketeer with an interest in audio and photographic products. A record of people management and range-building skills in a major multiple.

Senior Trade Marketer. £60,000 plus car. Highest calibre individual from a marketing or national accounts background with a top blue-chip FMCG manufacturer or retail buying experience. Top quality experience, together with a dynamic personality and strong interpersonal skills.

Sales promotion

Account Executive. c.£15,000. Energy, drive, commitment and a desire to get ahead in the agency world are the prerequisites in this exciting position. If you are a young graduate looking for a real challenge in a fast-growing sales promotion agency we are eager to hear from you. This is certainly not for a shrinking violet looking for an easy life!

Junior Account Manager. To £20,000. Opportunities like this don't come along very often. If you are an ambitious Account Executive or Junior Manager and would like to work on one of the most exciting travel/leisure accounts in the business, phone now.

Creatives. £Flexible. With a natural flair and an ability to challenge the status quo you also have real commercial awareness and the desire to make a difference.

Account Director. c.£42,000 plus car. With client-side FMCG experience to work with blue-chip clients. Excellent opportunity for a mature team player to contribute to future growth and their own career development.

Advertising

Account Executive. £16,000 plus benefits. You'll be working alongside one of the Company Directors, coordinating the daily running of accounts. Needless to say, you will need to be very accurate and show great enthusiasm.

Manager. £22,000 plus benefits plus car. Skilled in business-to-business and working on hi-tech accounts, you must have a good knowledge and understanding of direct response techniques, and be able to translate a client's problem into a clear, concise brief. You may have agency or client experience.

National Advertising Manager. To £25,000. A talented manager of national above-the-line activity. You will organise all press, radio and TV advertising on time, within budget and to an agreed marketing plan. You should have previous experience of working closely with agencies and production houses, media-buying skills and a clear under-standing of the latest developments in print and production technology.

Account Director. £32,000 plus car plus profit share. With full-service agency background to join a dynamic new hotshop.

Market research

Advertising Tracking Researcher. £25,000. If you have previous tracking experience or are currently working within advertising or marketing this position will be of interest. Confident and outgoing personalities are desirable to fit the current team. Will be handling top name brands.

Board Director. £Exc. package. Specialist agency requires a senior pharmaceutical professional with excellent track record. Both UK and international markets. Agency and client-side experience a definite advantage.

PR

PR Secretary/Receptionist. £11,000. Plenty of variety, including the opportunity to get involved in public relations projects for our household name clients. Keyboard skills, flex-ibility, organisational skills and the drive to get involved in many aspects of our business.

European Relations Officer. £17,500. Can you build on our links with France, Italy and Germany? Reasonably fluent in two of the principal EU languages, able to work on own initiative and with excellent organisational skills. You will be proactive in seeking EU funding, responsible for grant aid to relevant projects. Some evening and weekend work.

Press Officer. From £26,000. Responsibilities will include:

- ◆ maintaining and expanding relations with press and broadcast media, writing press releases and statements;
- ◆ advising senior management, individuals and committees on all aspects of press and media relations;
- ◆ raising awareness of the college's activities and publications through appropriate publicity and organising national press conferences and briefings.

Will have in-depth experience of press and media relations gained through at least five years in a similar organisation, excellent interpersonal skills, be able to communicate at all levels with tact and diplomacy. This is a job for a self-motivated, enthusiastic communicator.

Account Manager, Travel PR★. To handle travel and leisure accounts in our small, successful PR consultancy. Broad media contacts in business and consumer media and a minimum of five years' experience in consumer public relations. Creativity and ability to write news and feature copy, proven success in selling stories, energy and enthusiasm, the ability to work in a small team and juggle priorities.

Associate Director, Top 40 Agency★. Business-to-business, hi-tech and telecoms sectors. If you want to be stretched, challenged and rewarded with a board position in the next 18 months. This is a demanding role. You will have the full support of the board and the further resources of the parent plc, while retaining complete autonomy for both strategic and operational decision making.

★Salary is omitted here as this type of ad seldom mentions salary details.

Case Study

Tom needed work experience, but was caught in a catch-22 situation. He lived in the country, and there was no work locally – the nearest town was a two-hour bus journey away. To find work, he would have to buy a car or rent a flat – which would take all his earnings. His mother mentioned one day that Mrs Gore-Williams was organising a ball in aid of the Red Cross in the local hotel and that this hotel was looking for bar staff during the tourist season.

A few days later Tom had two jobs: one as part-time (paid) waiter four nights a week; and one unpaid as assistant to Mrs Gore-Williams. The waiting job was fun – tourists from abroad wanted to talk and ask his advice, and he learnt some useful background information for when he applied for tourism-related jobs.

Working with Mrs GW (as Tom called her) was an eye-opener. One minute he was phoning Buckingham Palace to check details of their royal guest, the next contacting PR agencies to ask if their clients would donate goods for the tombola. All extremely valuable experience and his Filofax was filling up with contacts.

On the night of the ball things went extremely well. Mrs GW was delighted with the amount of money the tombola raised. During the evening she introduced Tom to one of her guests, who asked searching questions about Tom's ambitions, then handed him his card and told him to get in touch. Reading it later on, Tom realised he was a senior executive in one of the largest advertising agencies. Networking can be the way into a job, provided you have something to offer.

Returners

Previous working experience can be helpful, whatever the job. This is especially true in the conference and events sector where maturity and life experience are very useful, so there is work for the 'more mature' person (male and female); if you have been out of work bringing up children, build on your consumer experience.

One way to restart is by taking temporary jobs in exhibitions or as an in-store demonstrator, and tell the companies you are looking for a full-time administration job.

Returners often need to update their image; cosmetics companies will often make you up before an important interview.

Women in Publishing has helpful one-day introductory courses, with networking opportunities. 'Creating your own Web Pages' and 'Freelancing in a Changing Industry' could be particularly useful. One of their trainees commented its course helped her to 'get a job I had little experience for, but knew I could do if given the chance – and I was'.

Top Tips

Networking is often the best way to find work. Belong to your local Chamber of Commerce, the Tourism Society, etc and go to meetings.

Useful contacts

Advertising Association, 15 Wilton Road, London SW1V 1LT (tel: 020 7828 2771)

Auralog (tel: 020 7929 6266)

Bureau of Freelance Photographers (BFP) (tel: 020 8882 3315)

Business Link (tel: 0845 600 9006; www.businesslink.org.uk)

CAM (Communication, Advertising and Marketing Education Foundation), Abford House, 15 Wilton Road, London SW1V 1NJ (tel: 020 7828 7506)

Career Development Loans (tel: 0800 585505)

Careers Helpline (tel: 0906 553 2056). The author helps with advice on getting into public relations or tourism marketing. Calls cost £1 per minute.

CHA (Corporate Hospitality Association) (tel: 01932 831441; www.eventmanager.co.uk)

Chartered Institute of Journalists (tel: 020 7252 1187)

Chartered Society of Designers, 29 Bedford Square, London WC1B 3EG (tel: 020 7407 9878)

CILT (Centre for Information on Language Teaching and Research) (tel: 020 7379 5110)

CIM (Chartered Institute of Marketing), Moor Hall, Cookham, Maidenhead, Berkshire SL6 9QH (tel: 01628 427 4990; www.cim.co.uk)

City and Guilds of London Institute (C&G), 1 Giltspur Street, London EC1A 9DD (tel: 020 7294 2468)

Corporate Events Association, Ferndene House, Windsor Walk, Weybridge, Surrey KT13 9AP (Sales@cha-online.com)

Department of Education, Northern Ireland, Rathgael House, Balloo Road, Bangor, County Down BT19 7PR (tel: 028 9127 9279)

DfES (Department for Education and Skills), Sanctuary Building, Great Smith Street, London SW1P 3BT (tel: 020 7925 5000)

Design Council, 28 Haymarket, London SW1Y 4SU (tel: 020 7839 8000)

Designers and Art Directors Association, 9 Graphite Square, Vauxhall Walk, London SE11 5EE (tel: 020 7582 6487)

Direct Marketing Association, Haymarket House, 1 Oxendon Street, London SW1Y 4EE (tel: 020 7291 3300)

ECCTIS 2000, Fulton House, Jessop Avenue, Cheltenham, Gloucestershire GL50 3SH (tel: 01242 518724)

Educational Grants Advisory Service, c/o Family Welfare Association, 501–505 Kingsland Road, Dalston, London E8 4AU (tel: 020 7254 6251)

Events Sector Industry Training Organisation (ESITO), Riverside House, High Street, Huntingdon, PE18 6SG (tel: 01480 457595)

Institute of Direct Marketing, 1 Park Road, Teddington, Middlesex TW11 0AR (tel: 020 8977 5705)

Institute of Journalists (tel: 020 7252 1187)

Institute of Sales and Marketing Management (tel: 01727 812500; www.ismm.co.uk)

Institute of Sales Promotion, Arena House, 66–68 Penton-ville Road, London N1 9HS (tel: 020 7837 5340)

IPA (Institute of Practitioners in Advertising), 44 Belgrave Square, London SW1X 8QR (tel: 020 7235 7020; www.ipa.co.uk)

IPR (Institute of Public Relations), 15 Northburgh Street, London EC1V 0AH (tel: 020 7253 5151)

Learn Direct (tel: 0800 100 900). Details on distance learning and other courses.

Learning and Skills Council (tel: 0845 019 4170; www.lsc.gov.uk)

London Chamber of Commerce and Industry (LCCI), Marlowe House, Station Road, Sidcup, Kent DA15 7BJ (tel: 020 8302 0261)

London Film School, 24 Shelton Street, London WC2H 9HP (tel: 020 7836 9642)

National Business Language Information Service (tel: 020 7379 5131)

National Council for the Training of Journalists (tel: 01279 430009; www.nctj.com)

National Express (tel: 08705 808080; www.gobycoach.com)

National Extension College, 18 Brooklands Avenue, Cambridge CB2 2HN (tel: 01223 400200; www.nec.ac.uk)

National Film and Television School, Beaconsfield Film Studios, Station Road, Beaconsfield, Buckinghamshire HP9 1LG (tel: 01494 731474; admin@nftsfilm-tv.ac.uk)

NUJ (National Union of Journalists) (tel: 020 7278 7916)

OCR (Oxford, Cambridge and RSA Examinations Board) (tel: 02476 470033; www.ocr.org.uk)

Open University (tel: 01908 653231; www.open.ac.uk)

Publishing Training Centre at Book House, 45 East Hill, London SW18 2QZ (tel: 020 8874 2718/4608)

QCA (Qualifications and Curriculum Authority) (tel: 020 7509 5555)

Scottish Office Education Department (tel: 0131 556 8400; www.butterworthscotland.com)

Scottish Vocational Education Council (SCOTVEC), Hanover House, 24 Douglas Street, Glasgow G2 7NQ (tel: 0141 248 7900)

Skill: National Bureau for Students with Disabilities, 336 Brixton Road, London SW9 7AA (tel: 0800 328 5050; www.skill.org.uk)

Small Business Services (tel: 0114 259 7788; www.sbs.gov.uk)

Student Loans Company Ltd, 100 Bothwell Street, Glasgow G2 7JD (tel: 0800 405010)

Trinity College Examinations Board (www.trinitycollege. co.uk; e-mail: brian.cooper@trinitycollege.co.uk)

UK ERASMUS Student Grants Council, The University, Canterbury, Kent CT2 7PD (tel: 01227 762712)

University and College Admissions Service (UCAS), Fulton House, Jessop Avenue, Cheltenham, Gloucestershire GL50 3SH (tel: 01242 227788)

Women in Publishing, c/o 78 Salop Road, London E17 7HT

11 Further reading

All books are published by Kogan Page unless otherwise stated.

Getting a job

Careers in Film and Video, R Ostrov and H Hall (1996)

Careers in Television and Radio, M Selby (1997)

Great Answers to Tough Interview Questions: How to get the job you want, M J Yate (1998)

How You Can Get that Job!: Application forms and letters made easy, R Corfield (1999)

Preparing Your Own CV, R Corfield (1999)

Marketing

Pocket Marketing, T Hindle and M Thomas (1994) Economist Books. Amusing introduction and comprehensive guide to 'marketing speak'.

Everything You Need to Know About Marketing, P Forsyth (1999)

How to Get on in Marketing, N Hart and N Waite (eds) (1994)

How to Market Books, A Baverstock (1999)

Customer Marketing: How customer marketing can increase your profits, J Curry (1998)

Marketing Communications, P R Smith and J Taylor (2001)

Practical Marketing, D Bangs (1993)

Advertising

The Advertisers Annual (Blue Book), published by Hollis. Currently this costs £210, so ask your college library to buy a copy, or look in your local library.

The New How to Advertise, K Roman and J Maas (1997), St Martin's Press

PR

Effective PR Management, P Winner (1993)

Getting into Journalism, V Reily Collins (Trotman, 1999)

Targeting Media Relations, D Wragg (1993)

The Essentials of Public Relations, S Black (1993)

Hollis UK Press and Public Relations Annual. An essential desk-top reference book. Phone 020 8977 7711 (www.hollis-pr.com).

The PR Business, Q Bell (1991)

Press Here! Annie Gurton's book on the PR industry is hard-hitting and laugh-out-loud funny in some places. Gives the low-down on how NOT to work – and sensible hints and tips on working effectively in PR. (Jossey-Bass Inc. Publishers, 1998.)

PR Planner. Phone 01494 797260 to order a copy.

Willings Press Guide. Phone 020 8977 7711 to order a copy.

Other useful publications

University and College Entrance: The Official Guide, published annually by UCAS.

Design Courses, published annually by Trotman/The Design Council.

Marketing and Sales and Advertising and Public Relations, careers leaflets available from the Central Services Unit for Graduate Careers and Research Advisory Centre, Crawford House, Precinct Centre, Manchester M13 9EP; should be available at your local careers office or a higher education careers service.

Getting into Advertising, The Advertising Association. (Send £5, contact details in Chapter 10.)

Graduate Careers in Advertising Agencies, Institute of Practitioners in Advertising (see Chapter 10 for contact details).

Waymaker publish a series of Editors Media Directories. Ask your college to subscribe (tel: 0870 736 0010; www.editorsmediadirectories.com).

Trade press

Campaign

Campaign Media Business (for media sales)

Marketing

Marketing Week

Mediaweek

press gazette

PR Week

www.prca.org.uk is a Web site to help companies search for suitable PR consultancies – you can use it to look for job leads!

Glossary

Here are descriptions of some words and phrases used in marketing and related areas, which sometimes have their own distinct meaning in these environments. Italics indicate a term explained in another entry in this glossary.

Above-the-line Advertising in the traditional media: press, TV, radio, cinema and outdoor (billboards, transport, etc). See *Below-the-line.*

Account Not to be confused with 'accounts' (number work). The piece of work an *agency* is working on, or the client it is working for, might be referred to as the account, eg the 'Bran Pops Account', the 'Sign Shop Account'.

Account manager The role that pulls everything together, selling, managing and liaising between the *client* and *agency* staff.

Agency Specialist firm where certain services can be bought, usually in one particular field such as public relations (PR) and often specialising in certain commercial areas, such as travel PR.

Agency producer The person in an advertising *agency* responsible for the production of a TV or film advertisement.

Animatics One stage on from *storyboards*: the film taken one more step as worked-up sketches on film with sound.

Art director The person in an advertising *agency* who takes charge of the visual side of an advertising *campaign*. Often works alongside a *copywriter*.

Assistant Usually personnel below *executive* level, perhaps not at professional level or still training.

Below-the-line All forms of advertising and promotion that are not *above-the-line*.

Blue–chip company A top public company.

Brainstorm A getting together of brains (with their owners) to come up with ideas, often for a product name or new *concept.*

Brand A particular type of product, such as the Pepsi brand of cola drinks.

Brief An instruction from a *client* on what needs doing; a description of their objectives, ideas and *budget.*

Budget The sum of money allocated to a particular project, to pay for all advertising, say, or the entire marketing of one brand.

Business-to-business As its name implies, this is communication or trade (including advertising) from one business to another, so not directed at individuals or the general public – not *consumer* advertising.

Campaign A marketing or advertising plan of action.

Cascade A marketing strategy in which a small market segment is targeted first, before the manufacturer 'cascades' into other markets.

Client The *organisation* (or its representative) that needs the service (advertising, market research, etc) and pays for it.

Concept The idea – often a visual one – behind the advertisement.

Consumer Ordinary person, who might buy *fast-moving consumer goods*, as opposed to industrial or other trade user.

Copy The words in an advertisement or the text of a press release.

Copywriter The person who thinks up the words for an advertisement: slogans, voice-overs, etc.

Cost-effective A *campaign* or promotion that will be financially beneficial, increasing sales so that the extra profit it generates is greater than the cost of the campaign.

Costings Working out the cost of the *campaign* or promotion.

Creative A person involved in the creative side of advertising (not the business, account handling or research sides). A creative department is where the ideas and plans are translated into visual images and words to communicate the message effectively.

Direct marketing and **Direct response advertising** Direct mail promotion and advertising, such as a coupon to fill in from a magazine or newspaper.

Director Usually a board director of a company in advertising, PR and similar circles, it can mean the person who controls a particular *account* or handles the *creative* process at a certain level (eg account director, art director).

Executive Usually means professional worker at a basic level, often at graduate intake level but after initial training. Account executive is a common job title.

Fast-moving consumer goods (FMCG) The name tells you what it is – not *business-to-business* goods or services, etc.

Firm, company Commercial *organisation* producing goods or services for sale.

Flyer One-page sales leaflet giving details of a product.

Fulfilment The process of dealing with an order or enquiry, from its receipt to delivery. This includes opening, processing, administration, packing and transport.

Gap in the market Where a particular market need has not been filled, leaving a commercial opportunity.

Graphic artist A trained specialist who might draw layouts, *storyboards*, etc. Often a first creative role in an advertising agency.

In-house Something, such as a market research project, done within the *organisation*, as opposed to being sent to an *agency* or consultancy to be done (out-of-house).

Launch Presenting the product or service for the first time in that campaign, with all the necessary publicity and advertising.

Market share The percentage of the market held by a particular *brand*, service or *organisation*.

Media The means of mass communication, such as TV and radio, the press, the Internet, etc.

Media buyer The person in an advertising *agency* who negotiates and buys advertising space or time. Sometimes a combined role with the *media planner*.

Media planner In an advertising *agency*, the person who draws

up a media plan incorporating media data, *campaign* requirements and liaison with the *client*, then books the media space: in
a large *agency* this is done by the *media buyer*.

Message The point that the *campaign* is aiming to get across to
the *consumer*.

Niche marketing Selling a product or service to a small,
narrowly defined market.

Organisation In this book, used to describe any company,
college, council, county, school, club, etc that might use
marketing skills. Could be referred to as 'the *client*' by personnel
in an *agency* environment.

Opportunity to see (OTS) Exposure on hoardings, etc.

Pitch Putting together a proposal for a *campaign*, from the
client's brief, and presenting it to the *client* (pitching), in the hope
of winning the business.

Planner Agency person who relates market research to the
end-user and applies this information, advising the *client*,
campaign *director, media planner*, etc.

Point-of-sale advertising As its name suggests, advertising to
a *consumer* already on the premises.

Production (the process, or the department) Physically
producing the advertisement, brochure, etc.

Product launch See **Launch**.

Research and development As its name suggests, the R & D
department create or adapt a product or service to fill a *gap in
the market*, as instructed by the marketing department.

Storyboards A series of boxes each containing a sketch.
Together they show the progress of a film sequence.

Tender When work is put out to tender, an invitation is offered
to *agencies* to *pitch* for the work.

USP Unique Selling Proposition or Unique Selling Point.

Viral marketing Any strategy that encourages individuals to
pass on a marketing message to others.

Index

Kogan Page *Careers in...* series

Careers Using Geography by Patrick Talbot
(0 7494 3069 9)
Careers Using Languages by Edda Ostarehild
(0 7494 2452 4)
Careers Working with Animals by Allan Shepherd
(0 7494 3644 1)
Careers Working with Children and Young People by Judith
  Humphries
(0 7494 3394 9)
Careers Working Outdoors by Allan Shepherd
(0 7494 3703 0)

All titles are available from good bookshops. To obtain further
information, please contact the publisher at the following address:

Kogan Page Ltd
120 Pentonville Road
London N1 9JN
Tel: 020 7278 0433
Fax: 020 7837 6348
www.kogan-page.co.uk